Natural **Disasters**

Hurricanes

by Kris Hirschmann

Lucent Books
San Diego, California

Titles in the Natural Disasters series include:

Avalanches

Earthquakes

Hurricanes

Plagues

Volcanos

On cover: The aftermath of Typhoon Nina in the Philippines.

Library of Congress Cataloging-in-Publication Data

Hirschmann, Kris, 1967–
    Hurricanes / by Kris Hirschmann.
      p. cm. — (Natural disasters)
    Includes bibliographical references and index.
    Summary: Discusses hurricanes, their birth and development, the devastation they can cause, and their aftermath.
    ISBN 1-56006-878-7 (alk. paper)
    1. Hurricanes—Juvenile literature. [1. Hurricanes.] I. Title. II. Natural disasters (Lucent Books)
    QC944.2 .H57 2002
    551.55'2—dc21

                                                    2001000569

Copyright © 2002 by Lucent Books, Inc.
P.O. Box 289011, San Diego, CA 92198-9011
Printed in the U.S.A.

Contents

Foreword

Fear and fascination are the two most common human responses to nature's most devastating events. People fear the awesome force of an earthquake, a volcanic eruption, a hurricane, and other natural phenomena with good reason. An earthquake can reduce multistory buildings to rubble in a matter of seconds. A volcanic eruption can turn lush forests and glistening lakes into a gray, flat landscape of mud and ash. A hurricane can lift houses from their foundations and hurl trucks and steel beams through the air.

As one witness to Hurricane Andrew, which hit Florida in 1992, recounts: "After the storm, planks and pieces of plywood were found impaling the trunks of large palms. . . . Eighteen-foot-long steel and concrete tie beams with roofs still attached were carried more than 150 feet. Paint was peeled from walls and street signs were sucked out of the ground and hurled through houses. Flying diesel fuel drums were a hazard, as were signs, awnings, decks, trash barrels, and fence posts that filled the skies. Mobile homes not only blew apart during the storm but disintegrated into aluminum shrapnel that became embedded in surrounding structures."

Fear is an understandable response to an event such as this but it is not the only emotion people experience when caught in the throes of a natural disaster or when news of one blares from radios or flashes across television screens. Most people are fascinated by natural forces that have the power to claim life, crush homes, tear trees from their roots, and devastate whole communities—all in an instant. Why do such terrible events as these fascinate people? Perhaps the answer lies in humanity's inability to control them, and in the knowledge that they will recur—in some cases without warning—despite the scientific community's best efforts to understand and predict them.

A great deal of scientific study has been devoted to understanding and predicting natural phenomena such as earthquakes, volcanic eruptions, and hurricanes. Geologists and seismologists monitor the earth's motion from thousands of locations around the world. Their sensitive instruments record even the slightest shifts in the large tectonic plates that make up the earth's crust. Tools such as these have greatly improved efforts to predict natural disasters. When Mt. Pinatubo in the Philippines awoke from its six-hundred-year slumber in 1991, for example, a team of scientists armed with seismometers, tiltmeters, and personal computers successfully predicted when the volcano would explode.

Clearly, the scientific community has made great strides in knowledge and in the ability to monitor and even predict some of nature's most catastrophic events. Prediction techniques have not yet been perfected, however, and control of these events eludes humanity entirely. From the moment a tropical disturbance forms over the ocean, for example, researchers can track its progress and follow every twist in its path to becoming a hurricane but they cannot predict with certainty where it will make landfall. As one researcher writes: "No one knows when or where [a catastrophic hurricane] will strike, but we do know that eventually it will blast ashore somewhere and cause massive destruction. . . . Since there is nothing anyone can do to alter that foreboding reality, the question is: Are we ready for the next great hurricane?"

The many gaps in knowledge, coupled with the inability to control these events and the certainty that they will recur, may help explain humanity's continuing fascination with natural disasters. The Natural Disasters series provides clear and careful explanations, vivid examples, and the latest information about how and why these events occur, what efforts are being made to predict them, and to prepare for them. Annotated bibliographies provide readers with ideas for further research. Fully documented primary and secondary source quotations enliven the text. Each book in this series provides students with a wealth of information as well as launching points for further study.

Introduction

A History of Destruction

In a letter to his father, fifteen-year-old Alexander Hamilton described two hurricanes he had experienced in St. Croix, West Indies, on August 3 and September 3, 1772:

> Good God! What horror and destruction! It is impossible for me to describe it or for you to form any idea of it. It seemed as if a total dissolution of nature was taking place. The roaring of the sea and wind, fiery meteors flying about in the air, the prodigious glare of almost perpetual lightning, the crash of falling houses, and the earpiercing shrieks of the distressed were sufficient to strike astonishment into Angels. A great part of the buildings throughout the island are leveled to the ground; almost all the rest very much shattered, several persons killed and numbers utterly ruined—whole families roaming about the streets, unknowing where to find a place of shelter—the sick exposed to the keenness of water and air, without a bed to lie upon, or a dry covering to their bodies, and out harbors entirely bare. In a word, misery, in its most hideous shapes, spread over the whole face of the country.[1]

These words were written more than two hundred years ago. But they could just as easily describe a hurricane and its aftermath today. Unrelenting wind, lightning, destruction, and the loss of life have been the hurricane's calling cards throughout time. Today, as much as ever, people around the world tremble at the approach of one of these great storms.

An Angry God?

The traditional fears are well founded. A hurricane is one of nature's most destructive forces. A strong hurricane can flood the lands, blow houses over, and fill the air with flying debris that can slice through skin and bone. It may spawn tornadoes and lightning that do their own brand of damage. And unlike a tornado, which strikes quickly and then departs, a hurricane may rage for days, wreaking havoc indiscriminately on everything in its path.

The sheer power of a hurricane is enough to strike terror into the bravest heart. But those who have lived through a hurricane note another dimension. Many people report that the hurricane comes to seem, somehow, alive. Nearly a century ago, renowned British author Joseph Conrad, who had spent years at sea in the days of sailing ships, put it this way: "An earthquake, a landslip, an avalanche, overtake a man incidentally, as it were—without passion. A furious gale attacks him like a personal enemy, tries to grasp his limbs, fastens upon his mind, seeks to rout his very spirit out of him."[2]

People were taking the hurricane's ravages personally long before recorded history. The word *hurricane,* in fact, comes from

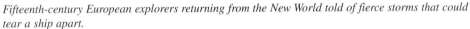
Fifteenth-century European explorers returning from the New World told of fierce storms that could tear a ship apart.

"Hurican," the name of the Carib god of evil. Caribbean peoples once believed that hurricanes sprang from the hand of a furious deity. This view is hardly surprising, considering that these storms arrived out of the blue and did untold damage. Hurican must have been very angry indeed to send such a punishment.

Naming the Beast

Hurican's realm, though, was limited. His influence did not extend to Europe, where hurricanes were unknown until the late 1400s. Around this time, Christopher Columbus and other famous explorers set sail in search of treasure and adventure around the globe. These explorers returned from their travels bearing tales of dreadful storms with winds strong enough to tear a ship to pieces and whip the ocean into a churning range of mountainous waves. Because the Caribbean was a popular destination at the time, the islanders' term for the killer storm was adopted in Europe.

The Americas were eventually settled by Europeans. As a result, variations of the word *hurican* settled into common usage in this region of the world. But different cultures around the world have

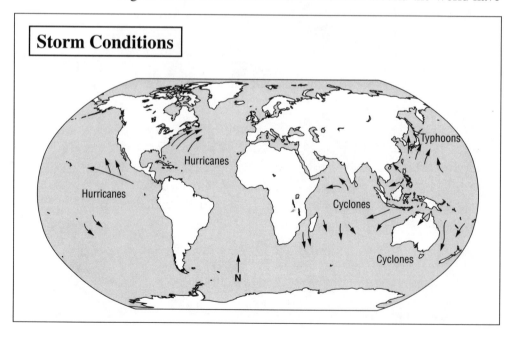

Storm Conditions

their own names for the beast. In China, the storm is known as a typhoon (from *ty-fung,* meaning "great wind"). In the Philippines, it is sometimes called a *baguio;* in Japan, a *reppu;* in Arabia, an *asifat.*

Weather forecasters in English-speaking countries use just three terms. The word *hurricane* (used in this book as a generic term) refers to storms that originate over the North Atlantic or eastern North Pacific Oceans. The word *typhoon* describes storms formed in the western North Pacific Ocean. And the word *cyclone* is used when a storm is born over the Arabian Sea, the Bay of Bengal, the Indian Ocean, or the coastal waters of Australia. Any of these storms may also be called a "tropical cyclone."

A Killer by Any Other Name

Although its name may change from place to place, the hurricane's essential character does not. Whatever label it bears, a hurricane brings destruction.

Thanks to technological advances such as satellites, radar, and specially equipped airplanes that can fly into the raging heart of the hurricane, forecasters are now able to sound the alert when these storms approach. This is a big improvement over the days when hurricanes arrived with little or no warning, taking people by surprise and killing thousands, or in some cases, hundreds of thousands. An untold number of lives have been spared because of this relatively new forecasting ability.

All the warnings in the world, though, cannot change the nature of the hurricane. Humankind's best efforts have failed to reduce the hurricane's winds, alter its path, or lessen its destructive powers. Many believe that it is possible to gain a greater understanding of hurricanes by studying them. But any insight that scientists may gain is unlikely to deter the threat. In the end, the only real solution is to get out of the way.

A Storm Is Born

For all their violence, hurricanes are the product of the calmest imaginable conditions: a flat sea, bright sunlight, gentle breezes, and a cloudless sky. These elements bring to mind a tropical paradise. But in the right circumstances, they can combine to produce nature's most powerful storms.

Warm, calm days at sea are common during certain parts of the year. Hurricanes, on the other hand, are not especially common, even when weather conditions seem to be favorable for their development. As one expert points out, "Since an annual average of only 99 tropical cyclones was observed globally over the period 1952–1971, these storms are relatively rare weather events."[3] Many factors must be in place before a pleasant stretch of ocean can evolve into a hurricane.

Hurricane Season

In the United States and Canada, the phrase "hurricane season" refers to the period between June 1 and November 30. The vast majority of hurricane activity, however, occurs from August through October, with storm frequency peaking in early to mid-September. Occasionally a storm may strike outside of season, but this rarity occurs perhaps once every few years.

Warm water is the trigger for hurricane season. As summer approaches, the sun's rays strike the earth with more concentrated force. Day after day, the oceans bask in the hot sun. Little by little, the winter-chilled waters heat up.

Heat is a form of energy, and heat energy drawn from the ocean is the hurricane's fuel. During the cold winter months, the ocean cannot provide enough fuel to power a hurricane. But during the summer, the temperature of the ocean waters may reach or exceed 80 degrees Fahrenheit. At this point there is enough energy available to create and sustain a hurricane.

Water temperatures peak at different times of the year in different parts of the world. For this reason, hurricane season is not the same in every region. In the northwest Pacific, for example, hurricane season is longer, lasting from May to December. In Australia the season runs from December to March, peaking in January and February. And the Bay of Bengal, near India, experiences two hurricane seasons each year: one from May to June and another from September to November.

The Wind Begins to Blow

Warm water by itself does not generate hurricanes. In order for a storm to get its start, the wind must blow.

Warm summer waters in the tropics combine with wind to fuel hurricanes.

All wind starts with the sun. The sun's rays travel through the earth's atmosphere and warm the land and sea below. Some of this warmth escapes into the air, heating it up. The amount of energy provided by the sun varies from place to place. Therefore the air acquires more heat in some places than in others.

Air expands and rises as it heats up. Its pressure also drops. Masses of high-pressure air always move toward areas of low-pressure air, so the cooler (higher-pressure) air surrounding a warm pocket rushes forward. This shifting air is felt as wind. Without differences in air pressure, wind would not exist—and neither would hurricanes.

Tropical Disturbances

A hurricane starts its life as an unremarkable weather event called a tropical disturbance. A tropical disturbance may be defined as "an area of enhanced cumulonimbus activity without a well-defined closed surface wind circulation."[4] In other words,

Cumulonimbus clouds piled up by opposing ocean winds cause a tropical disturbance, a weather system that can grow into a hurricane.

lots of cumulonimbus clouds—the towering, puffy type often seen on a hot summer afternoon—are building up, but they are just sitting there. They have not started moving together in the characteristic circular pattern of a hurricane.

The clouds of a tropical disturbance form over the ocean in areas of low-level wind convergence. "Convergence" means that air is "piling up" in a certain region because winds are blowing toward each other. "Low-level" means that this convergence is happening at or near sea level. The extra air has to go somewhere. It cannot go down; that direction is blocked by the ocean waters. It cannot go sideways; the wind is blowing inward. Its only option is to rise, so up it goes.

The rising air carries a great deal of moisture it has collected during its travels over water. This moisture is invisible at sea level. But the cooler a mass of air becomes, the less water vapor it can hold. As the air over a convergence rises and cools, some of the moisture it carries changes from invisible water vapor to visible water droplets. This process is called condensation, and it is a great creator of energy.

A tiny bit of energy is released every time a water droplet forms. When millions upon millions of droplets form, two things happen. First, the drops mass together and become visible as clouds. Second, the released energy generates thunderstorms. David Fisher, science writer and professor in the University of Miami's geology department, explains it this way: "As the air rises and cools and the water spills out into liquid droplets, latent heat is released. The developing thunderstorm uses this tremendous release of energy to power itself into a lightning-throwing monster."[5]

A collection of thunderstorms is not officially considered a tropical disturbance until it has held together for at least twenty-four hours. At this point forecasters start to keep a closer watch on the developing system. It is now considered a hurricane seedling.

Hurricane Conditions

Such seedlings come and go rather frequently during hurricane season. Only about half of these weather systems will become anything more than thunderstorms. Or, as one scientist puts it, a tropical disturbance has "about a 50/50 chance of making it to the big time—hurricane strength."[6] Particular conditions must exist before a disturbance can intensify. Although it is likely that dozens of minor contributors play a role in the formation of a hurricane, scientists agree on several major factors.

First, the disturbance must occur in a trough, which is defined as a long area of low air pressure. Troughs occur along the Intertropical Convergence Zone (a region near the equator where Northern and Southern Hemisphere air masses meet) or along the boundaries of two large air masses of different temperatures. These troughs sometimes act as invisible channels for tropical waves. Tropical waves are traveling "spikes" of low-pressure air that are hotbeds of rain activity. Under the right conditions, a small atmospheric push can rather quickly turn a tropical wave into a full-blown storm.

Second, the disturbance must be traveling over water warmer than 80 degrees Fahrenheit. Except for the chilly South Atlantic Ocean, all the world's seas reach this temperature at some point in the year. South Atlantic waters seldom get warmer than 75 degrees Fahrenheit, so this region alone has no history of hurricanes.

Finally, the disturbance must occur in an area of weak vertical wind shear. Vertical wind shear is defined as the difference in speed and direction between surface winds and higher-level winds. Researcher Patrick Fitzpatrick does a good job of explaining this concept: "For genesis [storm origin] to occur the wind must be roughly the same speed and blowing from the same direction at all height levels in the atmosphere. . . . [When] winds change dramatically with height, the thunderstorms are 'torn apart' in different directions."[7]

If all of these conditions—the presence of a trough, warm water, and weak vertical wind shear—are present, it is likely that the tropical disturbance will intensify.

Falling Pressure

In the heart of the tropical disturbance, warm air continues to rise. It passes easily through the troposphere (the lowest layer of the earth's atmosphere). At a height of about ten miles, though, the air column hits the stratosphere, a stable layer that resists changes in temperature. The rising air cannot penetrate the stratosphere. Instead, it spreads out to all sides, forming a flat roof of clouds.

Under certain conditions, the air at the top of the column can be whisked away faster than air is being pulled in at sea level. This results in a difference of air pressure between the top and bottom of the column. The difference is called a pressure gradient.

As the pressure gradient becomes more extreme, activity in the storm system increases significantly. Warm air at sea level starts to rise faster, moving toward the lower-pressure area at the top of the column. This movement causes the air pressure at sea level, called barometric pressure, to drop even further. The higher-pressure air surrounding the convergence rushes inward at ever greater speeds to replace the warm air being sucked upward. Throughout the system, wind speeds increase steadily.

The system will continue to strengthen as long as the barometric pressure at the convergence continues to drop. The lower the pressure, the stronger the storm. In fact, scientists can reliably guess the strength of a storm simply by measuring the pressure in its center.

Starting to Spin

To develop toward hurricane strength, a tropical disturbance must begin to spin. All hurricanes spin. In fact, spiral motion is a defining characteristic of these storms. But what is the "push"

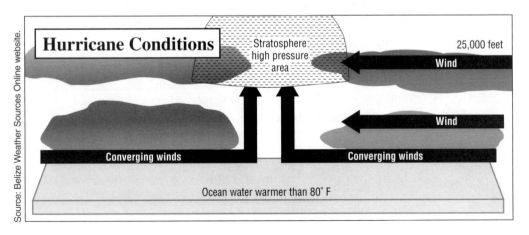

that causes a tropical disturbance to start swirling around the area of convergence? That push, it turns out, is supplied by the earth's rotation.

A bicycle spoke provides a good illustration of this concept. The spoke has two ends. One end is attached to the wheel's hub; one is attached to the rim. Every time the wheel makes a full revolution, the spoke also travels in a complete circle. But the circle traveled by the rim end of the spoke is much larger than the one traveled by the hub end. Therefore the rim end must move much farther and much faster than the hub end to finish one revolution in the same amount of time.

The rotation of the earth is very similar to the rotation of a bicycle wheel. Points along the broadest part of the earth—the equator—travel at top speed. Points near the poles barely move. All other geographic points on the planet fall somewhere between these two extremes of motion.

A satellite photo of a hurricane shows its characteristic spin, which is caused by the rotation of the earth.

The inequality in travel speed of different regions of the same planet has some interesting meteorological consequences. In particular, it can cause a windless mass of air to turn. This phenomenon occurs because the earth is spinning steadily in a counterclockwise direction, pulling the air mass along with it. If the air mass is located in the Northern Hemisphere, then the southern (equatorward) portion of the air mass is moving more quickly than the northern portion. In essence, the earth's rotation is giving the air mass a giant counterclockwise twirl. In the Southern Hemisphere exactly the opposite occurs. The northern portion of the air mass is closer to the equator and therefore moves more quickly than the southern portion. For this reason hurricanes that form south of the equator always spin in a *clockwise* direction.

This behavior is known as the Coriolis effect, after French physicist Gaspard de Coriolis, the first scientist to describe the force. The Coriolis effect occurs everywhere on earth except directly over the equator: When a weather system straddles this region, its top and bottom portions are moving at similar speeds, so it receives no "spin." A system must be entirely north or south of the equator before the earth's rotation gives it the push it needs to become a hurricane.

Getting Faster, Getting Stronger

A tropical disturbance that is located in an area ripe for hurricane growth receives its spin at the same time that high-pressure air is rushing in toward its center. This means that the system is both rotating and contracting (getting smaller). As long as these processes continue, the winds will get stronger and stronger, and the system will revolve faster and faster.

The intensification is due to a principle called conservation of angular momentum. Very simply put, this principle states that a spinning object will spin even faster if it becomes smaller. This acceleration occurs because a turning object has a certain amount of energy that cannot just disappear. If the object shrinks, the energy has to go somewhere, and it goes into increasing the object's speed.

Sailing Around the Storm

Not long ago, ships at sea were in terrible danger of accidentally wandering into a storm whose location defied prediction. But much changed with the understanding that hurricanes always rotate in the same direction. In his book *The Scariest Place on Earth*, David E. Fisher explains the effect of this knowledge on the seafaring community.

Since 1831, everyone has known that the winds of a hurricane blow counterclockwise. With this information it became possible for ships at sea to discern the location of distant hurricanes, and so to avoid them. Previously, a ship's captain feeling a strengthening wind in his face would naturally assume the storm was in front of him. But now he would know that if the wind was in his face, the hurricane generating it must lie to his right; if the wind came from his stern [rear], the storm must be to his left.

By 1944 this information was included in every seaman's training. Fisher quotes Ivan Ray Tannehill, a division chief of the U.S. Weather Bureau at the time: "The student navigator is told how to judge the location of the storm center, how to maneuver his ship to avoid it, and how to anticipate changes in the progressive movement of the storm so that he may alter his course accordingly." Today every competent seafarer knows how to avoid a hurricane at sea.

The same principle applies, for example, to a twirling ice skater. Writer and professor David Fisher elaborates: "A skater enters a spin with arms flung wide. . . . Without any further effort, she can increase her rate of spin simply by bringing her arms in and crossing them over her chest; she has decreased the distance of part of her body from the center of her rotation, and so without any expenditure of energy, her spin will speed up."[8]

It does not take long for a tropical disturbance to develop into an ominous, whirling system with steady winds. When the disturbance demonstrates consistent, closed-surface wind circulation, it becomes known as a tropical depression. And when winds in the depression reach sustained speeds of thirty-nine miles per hour (mph), the system is upgraded once again. It is now called a tropical storm. If nothing happens to slow or stop the storm's development, it will increase in violence—sometimes very quickly. A tropical storm can "spin up" rapidly under good conditions, with wind speeds increasing by 50 mph or even more in a single day.

Spiral Rain Bands

Inside the storm, winds are swirling toward the center of the system much as water swirls down a drain. One by-product of this process is cumulonimbus clouds, which form here and there throughout the system. These clouds may spawn thunderstorms that increase moisture and lower the air pressure. Such conditions are favorable for wind, so the spiraling air tends to flow through the stormy areas. This results in a kind of feedback loop. The wind creates clouds, which give birth to storms, which attract more wind, which creates more clouds. Before long the winds have become organized into spiraling paths. These paths are usually called rain bands because of the intense precipitation they generate. They are also sometimes called "feeder bands" because they "feed" heat and moisture into the hungry mouth of the storm.

Within the bands, winds travel briskly on their journey toward the center of the system. Rain, lightning, and other storm activity are at their most intense. Between the bands, though, sustained wind speeds drop dramatically, and rain activity becomes light and scattered. The bands themselves turn slowly along with the storm system. From above, the system resembles a giant pinwheel, spinning slowly in a breeze.

In a mature storm each rain band generally measures about 3 to 25 miles in width and about 8 to 300 miles in length. Although the bands may extend as much as 500 miles from the center of the storm, such a huge reach is rare; the radius of the average hurricane is around 150 to 200 miles.

The Calm Inside the Storm?

In *The Typhoon-Hurricane Story*, Robert E. Fuerst notes that the eye of a hurricane at sea is anything but calm:

Most people get used to thinking of the eye of the typhoon-hurricane as an area of calm, a quiet region, and may be misled into thinking of the sea surface of the eye in the same fashion—as a placid circle inside the violent seething water of the typhoon-hurricane proper. Such tales are pure and simple fiction, for the typhoon-hurricane eye is about the most dangerous place you can find on the ocean's surface. Waves of many different sizes exist; systems of waves are superimposed on each other or meet each other directly; every so often a wave of unusual size smashes through; and the general effect is one of utter confusion and chaos.

Fuerst quotes the account of a seaman on the *Idaho*, which was caught in the eye of an 1869 hurricane:

The waters . . . rose in their own might. Ghastly gleams of lightning revealed them piled up on every side in rough pyramidal masses, mountain high—the revolving circle of the wind, which everywhere enclosed them, causing them to boil and tumble as though they were being stirred in some mighty cauldron. The ship . . . rolled and pitched, and was tossed about like a cork. The sea rose, toppled over, and fell with crushing force upon her decks. Once she shipped immense bodies of water over both her bows, both quarters, and the starboard gangway at the same moment. Her seams opened fore and aft. Both above and below the men were pitched about the decks and many of them injured.

A Giant Eye Opens

Winds rushing through the spiral rain bands pick up speed on their inward journey, rising to a furious peak as they approach the center of the system. As sustained winds near minimum hurricane strength of 74 mph, the central rain bands suddenly part, opening a circular area of clear, calm air. Around this area, known as the eye, the storm continues to rage. But inside the eye, all is quiet.

The eye forms because near hurricane strength, winds cannot reach the actual center of the storm. One scientist compares the process to what one might feel in a speeding car: "As the driver makes a sharp turn, an 'invisible' force makes the driver lean outward. This outward-directed force . . . occurs because the driver's momentum wants to remain in a straight line, and since the car is turning, there is a tugging sensation outward. The sharper the

In the eye of a hurricane the sky is clear and the air is warm and still.

Wind and Waves

A hurricane at sea whips the oceans into a frenzy. In a strong storm, 30-foot waves are common, 50-footers come along with some regularity, and monsters measuring 70 to 100 feet from base to peak are not unheard-of. Waves of this magnitude tower above the decks of all but the grandest ships.

In his best-selling book *The Perfect Storm,* Sebastian Junger describes the water/wind interaction that creates these enormous waves:

> Heights of waves are a function of how hard the wind blows, how long it blows for, and how much sea room there is—"speed, duration, and fetch," as it's known. . . . A gale blowing across a thousand miles of ocean for sixty hours would generate significant wave heights of ninety-seven feet; peak wave heights would be more than twice that. Waves that size have never been recorded, but they must be out there. It's possible that they would destroy anything in a position to measure them.

> All waves, no matter how huge, start as rough spots— cats' paws—on the surface of the water. The cats' paws are filled with diamond-shaped ripples, called capillary waves, that are weaker than the surface tension of water and die out as soon as the wind stops. They give the wind some purchase on an otherwise glassy sea, and at winds over six knots, actual waves start to build. The harder the wind blows, the bigger the waves get and the more wind they are able to "catch." It's a feedback loop that has wave height rising exponentially with wind speed. . . . The seas generated by a forty-knot wind aren't twice as violent as those from a twenty-knot wind, they're seventeen times as violent.

curvature and/or the faster the rotation, the stronger is the . . . force."[9]

Instead of being flung outward as in this example, however, winds are flung upward when they get within ten to twenty miles of the storm's center. The roaring currents spiral skyward, creating a thick barrier of extreme violence around a miles-wide column of nearly motionless air.

This barrier is called the eyewall. In its mature state, the eyewall is an awe-inspiring formation, towering as much as fifty-thousand feet into the sky and ranging in width from 30 to 150 miles. From the outside the eyewall appears as a dark bank of boiling clouds that is briefly and randomly lit by flashes of lightning. Within the eyewall winds may blast at speeds of 150 mph or even more, whipping the seas below into a frenzy and carrying enough rain to turn the air into a nearly solid bank of water.

The Eye of the Storm

As the eyewall gains definition, the eye itself becomes calmer. Wind speeds drop dramatically and clouds disappear.

This effect is only partly due to the fact that winds cannot penetrate the center of the storm. A second factor is that the upward-rushing air in the eyewall creates a partial vacuum in the eye. As a result some of the flowing air reaching the top of the eyewall turns inward and sinks into the eye to fill the void. The sinking air becomes warmer as it approaches sea level. Warm air can hold more moisture than cold air, so the sinking air actually absorbs clouds as it gains heat. Before long most or all of the clouds have disappeared and the eye has become a stable region of still, warm air.

The eye of the hurricane is generally about twenty-five miles across, but it may be anywhere from ten to one hundred miles wide. Within this area the storm's barometric pressure is at its lowest and the temperature is at its highest; in fact, the air within the eye may be as much as 18 degrees Fahrenheit warmer than that in the eyewall.

A particularly well-developed eye can extend in a solid tube from the ground to the heavens. Those who have ventured into

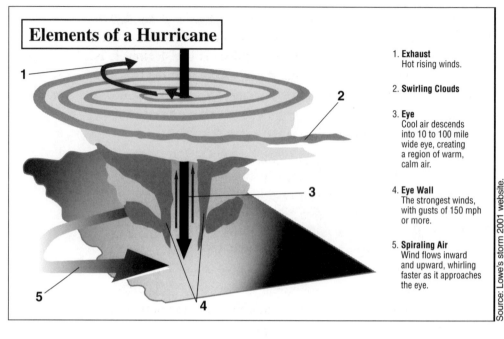

Elements of a Hurricane

1. **Exhaust**
   Hot rising winds.

2. **Swirling Clouds**

3. **Eye**
   Cool air descends
   into 10 to 100 mile
   wide eye, creating
   a region of warm,
   calm air.

4. **Eye Wall**
   The strongest winds,
   with gusts of 150 mph
   or more.

5. **Spiraling Air**
   Wind flows inward
   and upward, whirling
   faster as it approaches
   the eye.

Source: Lowe's storm 2001 website.

such an eye paint an amazing picture of the view within. A pilot recounts his memory of one long-ago hurricane: "Around us was an awesome display. [Hurricane] Marge's eye was a clear space 40 miles in diameter surrounded by a coliseum of clouds whose walls on one side rose vertically and on the other were banked like galleries in a great opera house. The upper rim, about 35,000 feet high, was rounded off smoothly against a background of blue sky."[10]

A Self-Sustaining System

Meanwhile, at the top of the eyewall, spiraling winds hurl themselves outward in all directions. Near the center of the hurricane, these spreading winds receive a strong push from the winds still exiting the eyewall. As they get farther from the center, however, these high-level winds cool and begin to lose momentum. Eventually they start to sink, falling around the outer edges of the storm. The now-calm air soon reaches sea level, where it promptly embarks upon a return journey into the heart of the hurricane. In this way, the system feeds itself.

At this point the storm that started its life as a sunny stretch of ocean has taken on a life of its own. It is now a hurricane with sustained winds that reach or exceed speeds of 74 mph. It is strong enough to do damage, but it is nowhere near the limits of its strength. The newborn hurricane continues to gulp as much energy as it can, and its hunger seems to have no end. Author Gary Jennings describes the fledgling hurricane:

> [It] is no longer a fragile thing that could be dispersed by a change in the weather conditions outside itself. It has become a self-contained, self-operating, self-perpetrating energy engine. The fresh air it devours from hundreds of miles around is its "fuel." The engine gulps it, warms it inside its hot chimney, rushes it upward, extracts its heat to keep the chimney hot, and spews out the used air as "exhaust" at the top of its chimney. . . . So long as it is over open sea where it can keep on devouring heat and moisture, the hurricane goes on getting bigger and stronger.[11]

Meteorologists will keep a close eye on the storm, constantly assessing its strength and its course. Although the newborn hurricane is still far out at sea, it is possible that it will travel toward land—and people.

Storm Watch

F̲ar from land, the hurricane has become a monster as much as a thousand miles across. The storm system rotates slowly, churning the ocean below into a nightmare landscape of mountainous waves. Winds roar toward the eye, carrying a dense mixture of rain and seawater torn from the crests of passing swells. Lightning flickers nearly continuously, thunder crashes, clouds boil, and the wind screams.

Some hurricanes never exceed minimum hurricane force. Others get stronger and stronger. But whatever their strength, all hurricanes have one thing in common: They are dangerous. As one seaman correctly points out, "There is no such thing as a 'small' or 'weak' hurricane. . . . Hurricanes are, by definition, the most powerful storms on this planet. Don't allow anyone to convince you otherwise. Any approaching hurricane places you and your vessel in immediate, grave danger."[12]

By the same token, a hurricane of any strength can wreak havoc on a populated area. If a storm approaches land, warnings should be raised in time to allow people to take necessary precautions. So although a hurricane at sea poses little danger to anyone other than a few unlucky sailors, meteorologists carefully track the storm's development and position.

Satellite Tracking

Hurricanes generally form far offshore in areas where the meteorologist's best information sources, including ships, radar, buoys, oil rigs, and submarines, are scarce. Therefore forecasters rely mostly on satellite images to provide data during the early stages of a hurricane.

The U.S. National Oceanic and Atmospheric Administration (NOAA) is one of several organizations globally that maintain weather-watching satellites. NOAA's GOES-8 satellite holds position over the Atlantic Ocean, continually gathering and transmitting images of the weather systems below. GOES-10 performs the same duty over the Pacific Ocean. By monitoring the images obtained through the GOES units and other satellites, meteorologists can keep track of a hurricane anywhere in the world long before it moves into a position to endanger human life.

It is not possible to know exactly how many hurricanes went unnoticed before the early 1960s, when satellite imagery first became available. The fact remains that forecasters catalog many more hurricanes today than they did a mere forty years ago. In fact, one author points out that "around the world today, meteorologists track about 100 tropical cyclones a year. Before the era of satellites, they were only able to find about half that

Satellite images help meteorologists pinpoint a hurricane's location and predict its course.

many."[13] These figures suggest that roughly half of all pre-1960s hurricanes were never detected.

Today, satellites serve as a meteorologist's "eyes in the sky," constantly monitoring the earth's weather systems and making it impossible for a developing hurricane to go unnoticed. For this reason, former National Hurricane Center director Robert Sheets has called satellites "the single most critical hurricane-watching device we have."[14]

Naming Hurricanes

Naming hurricanes is an important aspect of tracking them. Before the mid-1940s, forecasters identified hurricanes by their latitude

Atlantic Hurricane Names

2001	2002	2003	2004	2005	2006
Allison	Arthur	Ana	Alex	Arlene	Alberto
Barry	Bertha	Bill	Bonnie	Bret	Beryl
Chantal	Cristobal	Claudette	Charley	Cindy	Chris
Dean	Dolly	Danny	Danielle	Dennis	Debby
Erin	Edouard	Erika	Earl	Emily	Ernesto
Felix	Fay	Fabian	Frances	Franklin	Florence
Gabrielle	Gustav	Grace	Gaston	Gert	Gordon
Humberto	Hanna	Henri	Hermine	Harvey	Helene
Iris	Isidore	Isabel	Ivan	Irene	Isaac
Jerry	Josephine	Juan	Jeanne	Jose	Joyce
Karen	Kyle	Kate	Karl	Katrina	Keith
Lorenzo	Lili	Larry	Lisa	Lee	Leslie
Michelle	Marco	Mindy	Matthew	Maria	Michael
Noel	Nana	Nicholas	Nicole	Nate	Nadine
Olga	Omar	Odette	Otto	Ophelia	Oscar
Pablo	Paloma	Peter	Paula	Philippe	Patty
Rebekah	Rene	Rose	Richard	Rita	Rafael
Sebastien	Sally	Sam	Shary	Stan	Sandy
Tanya	Teddy	Teresa	Tomas	Tammy	Tony
Van	Vicky	Victor	Virginie	Vince	Valerie
Wendy	Wilfred	Wanda	Walter	Wilma	William

Source: National Hurricane Center website, www.nhc.noaa.gov/aboutnames.html

Eastern North Pacific Hurricane Names

2001	2002	2003	2004	2005	2006
Adolph	Alma	Andres	Agatha	Adrian	Aletta
Barbara	Boris	Blanca	Blas	Beatriz	Bud
Cosme	Cristina	Carlos	Celia	Calvin	Carlotta
Dalilia	Douglas	Dolores	Darby	Dora	Daniel
Erick	Elida	Enrique	Estelle	Eugene	Emilia
Flossie	Fausto	Felicia	Frank	Fernanda	Fabio
Gil	Genevieve	Guillermo	Georgette	Greg	Gilma
Henriette	Hernan	Hilda	Howard	Hilary	Hector
Israel	Iselle	Ignacio	Isis	Irwin	Ileana
Juliette	Julio	Jimena	Javier	Jova	John
Kiko	Kenna	Kevin	Kay	Kenneth	Kristy
Lorena	Lowell	Linda	Lester	Lidia	Lane
Manuel	Marie	Marty	Madeline	Max	Miriam
Narda	Norbert	Nora	Newton	Norma	Norman
Octave	Odile	Olaf	Orlene	Otis	Olivia
Priscilla	Polo	Patricia	Paine	Pilar	Paul
Raymond	Rachel	Rick	Roslyn	Ramon	Rosa
Sonia	Simon	Sandra	Seymour	Selma	Sergio
Tico	Trudy	Terry	Tina	Todd	Tara
Velma	Vance	Vivian	Virgil	Veronica	Vicente
Wallis	Winnie	Waldo	Winifred	Wiley	Willa
Xina	Xavier	Xina	Xavier	Xina	Xavier
York	Yolanda	York	Yolanda	York	Yolanda
Zelda	Zeke	Zelda	Zeke	Zelda	Zeke

Source: National Hurricane Center website, www.nhc.noaa.gov/aboutnames.html

and longitude positions. This was a very inefficient system. Since hurricanes move, a storm had to be described in different terms every time its location shifted. Moreover, it is not uncommon for several hurricanes to exist at the same time. Position-based names were not just cumbersome, they were also confusing when more than one hurricane was present in the same general area. The simple naming system that exists today is considerably more useful to meteorologists as they monitor a hurricane.

A weather system is named when it reaches tropical storm strength. The names are drawn in order from a standard, alphabetically ordered list. In most areas the first hurricane of the season receives a name starting with the letter *A*, the second with *B*, and so on. The 2000 Atlantic hurricane season, for example, began with Hurricane Alberto, tropical storms Beryl and Chris, and Hurricane Debby. In total, the season produced fourteen named storms, the last one being tropical storm Nadine in late October.

Most global hurricane regions (including the Atlantic, Australian, Northeast Pacific, Northwest Pacific, and Southwest Indian regions) maintain standard lists of hurricane names. Names are usually recycled—the same name may be used to identify more than one storm in an interval of several years. If a storm has particularly severe effects, however, its name is retired. Recent hurricanes whose names have been forever dropped from the list include Hugo (1989), Andrew (1992), Fran (1996), Mitch (1998), and Floyd (1999).

Measuring the Winds

Once a hurricane has been spotted and named, meteorologists turn their attention to measuring its strength.

Atlantic hurricanes are ranked on the Saffir-Simpson Scale, which assigns each storm a category from 1 to 5 based on its maximum sustained wind speed. A Category 1 storm is the weakest hurricane, with wind speeds ranging from 74 to 95 mph. In a Category 2 storm, winds range from 96 to 110 mph. A Category 3 storm is characterized by winds of 111 to 130 mph, and a Category 4 storm features wind speeds of 131 to 155 mph.

Hurricanes with sustained wind speeds over 155 mph are the true terrors of the natural world. They are classified as Category 5 storms, and they are strong enough to wipe the earth clean if they make landfall. Only two Category 5 storms—Camille in 1969 and the Florida Keys Labor Day Hurricane in 1935—have made U.S. landfall since the dawn of the twentieth century.

A hurricane's category is not fixed. It may change dozens of times before the storm has run its course. A typical hurricane intensifies slowly, going from a Category 1 to a Category 2 or perhaps 3 before losing strength. Occasionally, though, change may

The Fujiwara Effect

When two rotating storms get within about nine hundred miles of each other, they begin to affect each other's motion. Under the right conditions they will start circling each other, both spinning around a central point. This is called the Fujiwara effect after Dr. Sakuhei Fujiwara, the first scientist to describe the phenomenon.

In his *USA Today* article "Dance of the Storms," journalist Chris Cappella describes events of the busy 1995 hurricane season that called attention to the Fujiwara effect:

When Tropical Storm Iris was approaching the Windward Islands on August 23, 1995, and Hurricane Humberto was close behind, they drew close enough together to begin a Fujiwara dance. . . . As Humberto chased down Iris, Humberto began to lift northward over Iris while Iris slowed down and turned a bit to the south. Iris became a hurricane just as this "dance" began but both storms were weakened by their passion for each other. As they weakened, other forces in the atmosphere broke them apart and sent them on their separate ways.

About eight days later, Iris, now a hurricane with 110-mph winds, was moving northward east of Bermuda. This time Tropical Storm Karen scooted in behind Iris. But Karen was a much weaker storm with winds of only 45 mph. As the storms moved closer the Fujiwara effect began. But Iris' strength dominated and poor Karen was flung around Iris to the north. Iris absorbed Karen right into its circulation while barely flinching.

be rapid. Hurricanes have been known to increase from Category 1 or 2 to Category 4 or 5 within a day or two.

Category 3, 4, and 5 storms are collectively referred to as major hurricanes, with the potential to severely damage land, property, and life. Fortunately for the human population of the United States, storms of this strength make up only about 20 percent of all landfalling hurricanes. This 20 percent, however, accounts for more than 80 percent of all U.S. hurricane damage. Major hurricanes thus are always of great concern to meteorologists, who pay especially close attention to these weather systems throughout their life cycle.

Strength in Numbers

There is a good reason why major hurricanes are so much more dangerous than those in Categories 1 and 2. Whenever the wind's speed increases, its damaging power increases even more. A scientific explanation of this phenomenon is provided by a government meteorologist:

> Would a minimal 74-mph hurricane cause one-half the damage of a major hurricane with 148-mph winds? No. The amount of damage does not increase linearly with the wind speed. Instead, the damage produced increases exponentially with the winds. The 148-mph hurricane (a Category 4 on the Saffir-Simpson Scale) may produce, on average, up to 250 times the damage of a minimal Category 1 hurricane.[15]

Extending the illustration, a Category 5 hurricane packs at least twice the punch of a Category 4 storm. A hurricane of top magnitude therefore may be expected to do at least five hundred times the damage of a Category 1 storm. A heavily populated area would experience utter devastation if such a storm were to make landfall.

Interestingly, a hurricane's size has nothing to do with its strength. A very small hurricane can be incredibly powerful. Hurricane Andrew, a Category 4 storm that devastated south Florida in 1992, is a good illustration of this principle. With 145-mph sustained winds, Andrew was one of the strongest hurricanes ever to make landfall in the United States. But relative to most hurricanes, Andrew was tiny; its strongest winds extended only about fifty miles from its eye.

A hurricane's size, therefore, is not a primary concern. Meteorologists are much more concerned with monitoring its strength, and thus its category, which is so predictive of its damage potential.

An Eddy in a River

A hurricane's name and strength are meaningless if no one can predict whether and where it will make landfall. So the key pieces of information in tracking any hurricane are the exact location and direction of the storm.

A hurricane's path is determined by the large region of moving air, called the steering current, in which it is embedded. The

Despite its small size, Hurricane Andrew caused tremendous damage when it made landfall in Florida.

Exponential Versus Linear Growth

Wind's power, and therefore its damage potential, increases exponentially with its speed. But what does "exponentially" mean? To understand the concept, it is important to know the difference between linear and exponential growth.

In linear growth the same amount (call it x) is always *added to* a base number. The base number may be zero, a million, or any other number, but x never changes. A jigsaw puzzle provides a good example of linear growth. The person doing the puzzle adds one piece at a time, regardless of whether the puzzle is just begun or nearly completed.

In exponential growth, however, the base number is always *multiplied by* some amount. Cell division provides an example of exponential growth. One cell divides into two. Both new cells also divide, resulting in a total of four cells. The four cells become eight; eight become sixteen; and so on. Each increase is exactly double the one that came before. Clearly, exponential growth increases faster than linear growth.

The growth of winds to hurricane strength provides an even more impressive example of the power of exponential growth, since the bigger the base number, the greater the increase. And each time wind speed doubles, its power increases eight times. This means that if a wind blowing 10 mph has an imaginary "destruction rating" of 1, then a wind blowing 20 mph has a rating of 8 (1x8). Doubling the speed from 20 to 40 mph increases the rating to 64 (8x8), and doubling it yet again to hurricane speeds of 80 mph bumps the rating up to 512 (64x8). And a major hurricane with wind speeds of 160 mph rates an incredible 4096 on the destruction scale.

hurricane is blown along within the steering current much as a floating leaf is carried downstream by the waters of a brook. By studying the steering current, forecasters hope to predict the hurricane's track. This is not an exact science, however. It is difficult for meteorologists to pinpoint the course and speed of a hurricane even if they understand the steering current.

The problem is illustrated by Patrick Fitzpatrick's description of an eddy in a river:

> The river transports the eddy downstream. However, the eddy will not necessarily move straight because the speed of the current varies horizontally; for instance, it may be faster in the center and slower toward the river banks. As a result, the eddy may wiggle off a little to the left or right as it moves downstream and, depending on the situation, may speed up or slow down. Furthermore, the eddy's rotation may alter the current in its vicinity, which in turn will alter the motion of the eddy.[16]

Like the eddy in this example, a hurricane can move about within the steering current. Its rotation can also affect the very nature of the steering current, causing further changes in the hurricane's motion. And there is an additional complication for forecasters: Unlike the river in Fitzpatrick's example, a steering current can rapidly change its speed and orientation, carrying the hurricane with it.

Blocking the Path

Although the steering current plays the biggest role in determining a hurricane's general path and speed, other factors are involved. A traveling hurricane is subject to many other forces, the first of which is the rotation of the earth itself. The earth's counterclockwise spin provides a slight push westward and poleward. If nothing interfered with the earth's push, a Northern Hemisphere hurricane would drift slowly northward within the steering current; a Southern Hemisphere hurricane would drift southward.

But interference generally is present, in the form of the huge areas of high and low pressure that dot the earth's atmosphere. Depending on the time of year, the sun heats different parts of the planet to different degrees. As a result enormous ridges (areas of high pressure) and troughs (areas of low pressure) form in certain areas. These areas are consistent from one year to the next. A portion of the North Atlantic region, for example, always sits under an area of high pressure called the "Bermuda high" during hurricane season. Another ridge called the "North Pacific high" sits over the North Pacific Ocean. Still other ridges sit south of the equator. Collectively, these areas of high pressure are known as subtropical ridges.

Hurricanes are areas of low pressure. As such they cannot move into areas of higher pressure. They actually bounce off any ridge they encounter. So even though the earth's rotation nudges a hurricane poleward, a high-pressure ridge may act as a barricade that blocks its path.

Typical Paths

In the Atlantic Ocean hurricanes generally form south of the Bermuda high. Upper-level winds in this region blow toward the west. Under typical conditions, then, a hurricane is pushed westward along the bottom edge of the ridge. The storm would also drift northward if it could, but the ridge prevents it from doing so. After a while, however, the hurricane reaches the westernmost edge of the Bermuda high. No longer blocked by high-pressure air, the hurricane shifts course and begins curving northward along the edge of the ridge.

Wind conditions change near the top of the Bermuda high. At this latitude, upper-level winds blow toward the east rather than the west. When the hurricane gets far enough north, it catches a ride on a new steering current and starts moving back out to sea. This change of direction heralds the storm's death. Trapped over the chilly waters of the North Atlantic Ocean, the hurricane quickly loses strength and soon falls apart.

Storm systems that form off the coast of China in the northwest Pacific Ocean typically behave just like Atlantic hurricanes. They move westward at first, then swoop to the north and finally to the east. Hurricanes born in the South Indian Ocean (between Australia and Africa) also move to the west initially. But these hurricanes are phenomena of the Southern Hemisphere and are therefore subject to different forces than storms located north of

The Northeast Pacific Path

Many hurricanes form in the northeast Pacific Ocean, off the coast of Central America. Yet not one of these storms has ever hit the United States.

Two geographic factors keep the West Coast safe from hurricanes. One is the general east-to-west motion of the winds near the equator. Hurricanes that form west of the continental United States tend to be pushed even farther west by the steering current. This means that they usually drift harmlessly out to sea instead of toward land.

The second factor is the temperature of the water in this region. It is much too cold to provide the energy the hurricane needs to survive. On his "Frequently Asked Questions" web page, scientist Christopher Landsea describes the effect of this temperature drop: "Along the U.S. west coast, the ocean temperatures rarely get above the lower 70s, even in the midst of summer. Such relatively cool temperatures are not energetic enough to sustain a hurricane's strength. So for the occasional Northeast Pacific hurricane that does track back toward the U.S. west coast, the cooler waters can quickly reduce the strength of the storm."

The Hawaiian Islands were hit hard by Hurricane Iniki.

Even if a storm moves straight out to sea, cold water usually kills it before it gets far. Every few years, however, a hurricane makes it all the way to Hawaii. Such hurricanes seldom do much damage; they are too weak from their long journey across the chilly ocean. But a few, like Iniki, have been incredibly destructive. Hurricane Iniki struck Hawaii in September 1992. Small but intense, Iniki killed seven people and caused an estimated $1.8 billion in damage, making it one of the most devastating hurricanes ever to hit the United States.

the equator. Instead of moving northward along the edge of a subtropical ridge, Indian Ocean storms shift to the south before making their eastward turn.

Judging the Curve

In some regions of the world a hurricane's typical path tends to take it away from people. In other regions hurricanes tend to move toward inhabited areas. The expected path of an Atlantic hurricane, for example, often crosses the island nations of Barbados, Puerto Rico, Jamaica, Cuba, and the Bahamas, to name just a few—with the densely populated United States not far beyond. Guessing when an Atlantic hurricane will curve north is therefore one of the meteorologist's most important jobs. The position of the Bermuda high is a key factor in this guess. If the high sits far out over the open ocean, a hurricane may make an early turn to the north and avoid land altogether. If, on the other hand, the Bermuda high sits near the east coast of the United States, there is a good chance that the hurricane will eventually threaten populated areas.

David Fisher describes this principle: "If the high were a bit more extensive, or located a bit farther west, the storm could slam into the [U.S.] East Coast before turning. If the high were even more extensive, or farther west, the storm would sail past the southern tip of Florida before beginning its northward turn; it would then blow through the Gulf [of Mexico] and hit land somewhere along the Gulf Coast."[17]

Case Study: Hurricane Betsy

It would be easy to forecast a hurricane's path if areas of high pressure never changed their shape or position. Unfortunately, this is not the case. Global weather conditions can alter the shape of a ridge. They can also nudge a ridge a considerable distance in any direction. Any change in a ridge may affect the path of the hurricane. And because these changes can happen very quickly, meteorologists sometimes have a tough time predicting what a hurricane will do.

The path taken by Hurricane Betsy in September 1965 perfectly illustrates this problem. David Fisher describes Betsy's course:

She was following the classical hurricane track, heading due west but beginning to curve northward around the limits of the Bermuda high. . . . By September 5 she was about three hundred miles off the Florida coast, nearly even with Jacksonville. She looked to be heading up to hit the coast, perhaps around the Chesapeake Bay or, perhaps, to miss it entirely and curve around and fade away into the North Atlantic waters. But an unexpected low-pressure trough suddenly developed over the continental United States. This drew the Bermuda high to the west, placing it just north of Betsy, blocking her path.

Betsy changed her course and moved south toward Miami. At that point, Fisher continues, "she turned westward again, sailed over the Keys and into the Gulf, and then, turning north again, moved around the flank of the high. A few days later she blew into New Orleans, hitting the city with only a few days' warning, since the week before she had been heading in a completely different direction."[18]

Tourists in Florida battle blowing sand as Hurricane Gordon zigzags through the region.

Atypical Paths

A shifting ridge is not the only thing that can alter the path of a hurricane. Conditions within the hurricane itself can modify the surrounding weather systems, which may then lead to changes in the hurricane's direction. Very strong storms, for example, seem to be less affected by large ridges such as the Bermuda high. "A large storm has more bulk and consequently throws its own weight around, forcing the high to accommodate it,"[19] explains Jeffrey Rosenfeld. Rapidly intensifying storms may also be less affected by surrounding forces.

Weakening storms, on the other hand, are unusually sensitive to their environment. The slightest change in conditions can send these storms wandering willy-nilly across the map. Rosenfeld cites the example of 1994's Hurricane Gordon, which "took a bizarre S-shaped path from Central America to eastern Cuba and back to the Gulf before crossing the Florida peninsula on a northeasterly track. It accelerated out over the Atlantic in what seemed to be its final throes . . . [but then] made an about-face and looped back toward Florida and South Carolina."[20]

Although Gordon's path was unusual, the general situation was not. Hurricanes very seldom behave exactly as meteorologists predict. Storms regularly zigzag, do loop-the-loops, and reverse their course unexpectedly. Forecasting a hurricane's path can therefore be a frustrating guessing game in which predictions change from minute to minute.

Giving an exact prediction is less crucial when a hurricane is far out at sea. But the stakes increase dramatically when the storm draws within striking distance of land. People who may be affected by the storm need to know where the hurricane is going and what it is doing. So forecasters shift into high gear, using every tool at their disposal to monitor the storm around the clock. The information they provide may mean the difference between life and death.

The Hurricane Approaches

"**B**igger, Stronger, Closer," blared the headline on the front page of the August 23, 1992, edition of the *Miami Herald*. The accompanying article summarized information about the first hurricane of the season—a small but strong storm named Andrew that was getting way too close for comfort:

> Hurricane Andrew grew in strength and speed Saturday night. Forecasters issued a hurricane watch from Key West to Titusville as the storm chewed its way across the Atlantic toward the heavily developed South Florida coast. The leading edge of the storm could hit South Florida by tonight, said forecasters. . . . A high-pressure system off Georgia and the Carolinas is expected to keep the storm heading toward South Florida, instead of veering north as many hurricanes have in recent years.[21]

But no one, including the scientists tracking the storm, knew exactly what would happen. As the National Hurricane Center's Herb Lieb told an interviewer at the time, "Remember, we don't know if the atmospheric conditions near the storm are going to change any. If they do, the storm could veer away from us. That could happen any minute."[22]

This local newspaper coverage perfectly communicates the delicate balance of information and uncertainty that is the essence of hurricane prediction. It is nearly impossible to know for sure what a hurricane is going to do more than twenty-four hours in advance. But to the people in the path of the storm, every hour counts. Forecasters therefore do their best to issue accurate and timely information.

The National Hurricane Center

In the United States, the National Hurricane Center (NHC) is at the heart of this effort. Based just outside of Miami, Florida, the NHC is responsible for tracking and forecasting hurricanes in the North Atlantic Ocean, the Caribbean Sea, the Gulf of Mexico, and the eastern North Pacific Ocean.

Most of the time, the NHC functions as a training and research facility. But the organization shifts into high gear when a hurricane looms on the horizon. Author David Longshore describes the atmosphere: "Round-the-clock shifts are established among NHC staff as a constant watch is placed on the system, designed to detect major changes in the storm's course and intensity within an hour of their occurrence."[23]

The flood of data obtained by the NHC is assembled into written advisories on a hurricane's strength, position, speed, and direction. These advisories are then issued to TV and radio stations, newspapers, magazines, and any other media outlet that can get the word out. A new advisory is issued every six hours throughout the lifetime of the storm. If the NHC detects a significant change in the storm, however, it will issue a special bulletin in addition to its regular advisories so that people can act on the most up-to-date information.

The NHC gets some of its information from NOAA's GOES satellites. It also relies on a host of land- and sea-based data sources, including buoys, ships, and a high-tech Doppler radar network that stretches from the Gulf Coast of Mexico to southern Canada. These sources provide good general information about a hurricane, but for precise data, it is necessary to physically enter the storm.

Flying into the Storm

The NHC employs a fleet of ten airplanes for this purpose. The fleet is maintained and manned by the U.S. Air Force Reserve's 53rd Weather Reconnaissance Squadron, also known as the Hurricane

Hunters. The Hurricane Hunters' airplanes are equipped with an array of weather instruments that can measure wind speed, air pressure, temperature, and other important aspects of a hurricane.

The job of the Hurricane Hunters is to determine the precise location, motion, strength, and size of a storm, then transmit this information back to the NHC for analysis. To get this information, a Hurricane Hunter airplane flies back and forth within the hurricane in a giant X pattern, passing through the eye once every two hours or so. A typical mission lasts ten hours. When one crew's shift ends, another plane slips into place and continues the surveillance pattern, thus ensuring that the hurricane is monitored around the clock.

NOAA's Aircraft Operations Center is another valuable source of hurricane information. The AOC maintains three hurricane-monitoring airplanes that boast even more instruments than the

Hurricane Hunters fly back and forth through a hurricane, transmitting critical data to the National Hurricane Center.

Into the Eye

On July 23, 1943, Colonel Joseph Duckworth of the U.S. Army Air Corps became the first pilot to fly into the heart of a hurricane. For their article "The 1943 'Surprise' Hurricane," authors Lew Fincher and Bill Read interviewed Lieutenant Ralph O'Hair, Duckworth's navigator on that historic flight, and summarized his memories of the experience.

As they approached the storm at a height of between four thousand to nine thousand feet, the air became very turbulent. . . . [O'Hair] described the flight now as like "being tossed about like a stick in a dog's mouth." The rain was very heavy as they flew through the darkness, fighting the updrafts and downdrafts. Suddenly they broke into the eye of the storm. . . . The sky was filled with bright clouds and it seemed that they were surrounded by a shower curtain of darker clouds. As they looked down they could see the countryside. . . . The eye seemed to be about nine or ten miles across and they circled inside. As they exited the eye, the dark overcast and heavy rain again pounded them until they made their way out of the storm.

As they arrived back at the field, the weather officer, Lieutenant William Jones Burdick, asked to be flown into the storm, so O'Hair jumped out and the weather officer flew off into the hurricane with Duckworth. After that flight, [air force base] Bryan Field became a Mecca for Allied pilots wanting to learn the fine art of "instrument flying."

Hurricane Hunters fleet. Because they provide such detailed data, the AOC planes are especially useful in situations where a hurricane is threatening landfall.

Both fleets are essential links in the hurricane forecasting chain. As the Hurricane Hunters point out, "Studies have shown that the high accuracy data from our Air Force Reserve and NOAA aircraft have improved the forecast accuracy by about 25%. Aircrews in these storms also have detected sudden, dangerous changes in hurricane intensity and movement, which are currently very difficult to detect by satellite alone."[24]

Track Prediction Models

Back at the NHC the information obtained via surveillance airplanes and other sources is fed into computers. The computers run the data through a variety of models designed to predict the path and intensity of the hurricane.

The NHC uses a variety of computer models. The simplest type is purely statistical. It compares the current hurricane with past hurricanes and makes a guess based on that comparison alone. Dynamical models are more complex. They feed actual atmospheric data from a hurricane into physics equations that, when solved, yield a projected path. The most sophisticated models available combine statistical and dynamical information to make predictions.

No particular method is consistently better than the rest. Forecasters therefore hedge their bets by running hurricane data through several models, then using their own experience and expertise to choose the best answer. This process, however, is far from scientific. David Fisher grumbles that it is suspiciously like gambling: "It's like talking to five different touts at a racetrack, each one giving an inside tip on a different winner. When one of them wins, you kick yourself for not having listened to that particular tout, but if you listen to him next time, you'll probably lose your money."[25]

As a storm gets closer to land, however, computer models tend to agree more and more. At some point it becomes obvious that a hurricane will make landfall, and the public warning system grinds into motion.

Hurricane Warning

An area that is threatened by a hurricane will initially be placed under a hurricane watch. This means that a storm is approaching that may or may not affect that specific area. A hurricane watch is the NHC's way of telling people to stay alert and to pay close attention to weather bulletins.

Track predictions become increasingly accurate as the hurricane draws closer. By the time the storm is twenty-four hours away, the NHC has a good idea where it will make landfall. Stronger statements can now be issued. Areas likely to experience the outskirts of the hurricane will be placed under a gale warning (sustained winds of 39 to 54 mph are expected) or a storm warning (sustained winds of 55 to 73 mph are expected). Areas squarely in the path of the eye and the eyewall will be placed under a hurricane warning, which means that hurricane-force winds are expected to strike within twenty-four hours.

Danger in Front

Even within the eyewall, some areas of the hurricane are more dangerous than others. The front right quadrant (relative to the storm's direction of travel) is unquestionably the deadliest part of the hurricane. In *The Killer Storms*, author Gary Jennings explains why this is so.

Suppose that a hurricane [with wind speeds of 150 mph] is being pushed by a 40-mph wind behind it. Around the right-hand edge of the storm's circle, its own wind of 150 mph is augmented by the 40-mph wind which is moving the whole storm system. In other words, the combined winds have an impact of 190 mph. On the left-hand edge of the hurricane, however, its own wind is blowing backward against the wind that's pushing the storm. If the following wind's 40 mph is subtracted from the hurricane's 150 mph, the effective wind force on that side is only 110 mph. This is still a punishing, destroying, killing wind. But plainly, if there is *any* "safer" side to a hurricane, it is the left rather than the right.

Televised status reports from the National Hurricane Center provide vital information about a storm's course and intensity.

The media plays a very important role in getting these warnings out to the general public. TV, radio, and print organizations take the NHC advisories and broadcast the information on a regular basis. If a hurricane is very close or very dangerous, many TV stations will even suspend their regular programming to air continual hurricane coverage.

Damage Potential

The amount and kind of media coverage varies depending on the intensity of the coming storm. A hurricane's category designation is a reliable predictor of its damage potential, and media outlets gear their information accordingly.

The weakest hurricane, a Category 1 storm, usually damages plant life such as trees and shrubs. It may also produce floods and tear small boats from their moorings. It may do some damage to unanchored mobile homes. But most structures will not be harmed by a Category 1 hurricane. Local residents whose homes are not located in a flood-prone area often are advised to ride out the storm.

A Category 2 storm can be expected to cause major damage to mobile homes and minor damage to other structures. Flooding also can be expected two to four hours before the arrival of the eye. When a hurricane of this strength approaches, government officials advise people in shoreline residences and low-lying areas to evacuate.

Major hurricanes pose increasingly severe risks to land and property. A Category 3 storm (such as Fran in 1996) can cause widespread flooding and some structural damage. Category 4 storms (such as Hugo in 1989 and Andrew in 1992) can destroy mobile homes and cause extensive damage to other structures. And a Category 5 storm (such as the Florida Keys Hurricane of 1935) will be devastating. The Saffir-Simpson Scale describes the expected effects of a Category 5 hurricane:

> Shrubs and trees blown down; considerable damage to roofs of buildings; all signs down. Very severe and extensive damage to windows and doors. Complete failure of roofs on many residences and industrial buildings. Extensive shattering of glass in windows and doors. Some complete building failures. Small buildings overturned or blown away. Complete destruction of mobile homes. Major damage to lower floors of all structures less than 15 feet above sea level within 500 yards of shore. Low-lying escape routes inland cut by rising water 3 to 5 hours before hurricane center arrives.[26]

Preparing for the Storm

Whether the approaching hurricane is a weak Category 1 or a killer Category 5, preparations are necessary. As a hurricane approaches, residents of threatened areas brace themselves and their property against the assault.

Getting ready for even a minimal hurricane takes a lot of work. The American Red Cross, one of the most prominent U.S. disaster-management agencies, recommends a long list of actions, including the following: Prepare your property for high winds (which includes bringing light objects inside, trimming dead branches off trees and bushes, and boarding up windows); fill your car with fuel in case gas stations are destroyed during the storm; stock up on prescription medications; store valuables in a watertight container at the highest level in your home; turn off your water and electricity; turn off propane tanks; unplug small appliances; stock up on flashlights and batteries; and fill your bathtubs and sinks with clean water in case the public water supply becomes contaminated.

Even in a weak hurricane, homes in flood-prone areas can be severely damaged.

Protecting Your Pets

What happens to pets when a hurricane threatens? On the Ferret Friends Disaster Response International website, author Christine Winter describes the problem.

Most public shelters won't accept animals, forcing tough choices upon pet owners in evacuation zones. Disaster planners, to their dismay, are discovering that many pet owners with no place to go with their animals decide to stay in the path of the storm or load their pets into their cars and drive inland, contributing to dangerous gridlock. . . . [One resident] survived 1992's Hurricane Andrew in a darkened bedroom with her husband and four trembling dogs while the walls rattled around them. "There was no way I could drive away and leave my animals," [she] said, "and there was nowhere to go with them, so we stayed."

Florida was the first state to include animals in its disaster-planning process. . . . Most counties fulfill their duties by offering lists of pet-friendly hotels and kennels and veterinary clinics that will board animals during a disaster . . . [but] nobody certifies these kennels and vets' offices to make sure they are safe against hurricane winds or flooding.

Pets should always be included in a family's disaster plan.

Commercial pet shelters do exist. But like human shelters, they offer limited space and questionable protection. The Red Cross therefore recommends that animal owners use pet shelters as a last resort. A better approach, says the organization, is to create an advance evacuation plan that includes the family pets. As author Sybil Fix of the *Charleston Post and Courier* points out, "Friends who might otherwise frown seeing you show up with your three Labs or four cats will probably not mind it too much in the case of a disaster."

On paper, these instructions sound simple enough. But in practice, an approaching hurricane often sparks near-hysteria. Area residents mob the aisles of home improvement stores, grabbing plywood to board up their windows. Long lines of cars form at gas station pumps. Grocery store shelves are stripped of bottled water, flashlights, charcoal, canned food, and other necessities. People become frantic and angry as they race against the clock to protect themselves from the coming storm.

Evacuation

If the hurricane threat is deemed especially severe, the population may be asked to evacuate. Some people ignore this request, but they do so at their own peril. As the American Red Cross points out in its educational materials, "Local officials advise leaving only if they truly believe your location is in danger, so it is important to follow their instructions as soon as possible."[27]

"As soon as possible" is a key part of this advice. Roadways were not designed to be used by every area resident simultaneously. A major evacuation can clog highways, turning them into virtual parking lots where cars may sit without moving for hours on end. People who try to leave their homes at the last minute may find that they are not going anywhere, after all.

Even if evacuation recommendations are followed, it is possible that many will be caught by the hurricane. Many areas, including hurricane-prone Florida, simply cannot accommodate a mass evacuation. "State emergency-management officials concede that in almost every region of the state, there may not be enough warning time to effectively evacuate everyone vulnerable to an approaching hurricane," writes hurricane expert Jay Barnes. If a major hurricane makes landfall during such an evacuation, he says, "The risk is great that more people would be killed in their cars than in their homes."[28]

Storm Shelters

Those who cannot leave or who choose not to leave may turn to emergency storm shelters. Local Red Cross chapters organize and run such shelters, which are usually located in high school gymnasiums or other large, sturdy structures with bathroom facilities.

They are not comfortable, but they do provide some protection for people with nowhere else to go.

A Florida newspaper article describes what to expect when seeking refuge in a hurricane shelter:

> Go to a shelter as soon as an announcement is made that it is open; space is limited. Hundreds of other people will be in the shelters, so be prepared to live with strangers at close quarters for an indefinite period of time. Shelters tend to be barren. Most creature comforts must be carried in by the visitor. Some shelters will have food, others will not. It is best to bring your own. And don't expect to find a bed. Be ready to set up a home away from home on the floor.[29]

Despite the spartan conditions, many people prefer hurricane shelters to staying at home. Shelters are sturdier than most private residences, and it is comforting to be with other people when a hurricane strikes.

But even an official shelter may not be safe during a hurricane. One author describes the frightening scene that occurred when floodwaters reached a shelter during Hurricane Hugo:

> Out of the darkness came the big, black, silent wave crashing into the school. The wave slammed into the east side of the building with so much force it pushed the air conditioning and heater units right out of their casements. At first the noise was low and muted and was felt more than it was heard, but the building shook as if an earthquake had struck. . . . A solid foot of water came cascading down the halls and into the rooms. . . . The foot of water was suddenly a foot and a half and then two feet, and everyone was screaming and holding on to one another and anything they could grab.[30]

Because shelters cannot guarantee safety, and because the space inside is so limited, they are usually recommended only as a last resort.

Riding It Out

Some area residents completely ignore hurricane warnings, neither preparing their homes nor evacuating, even when a risky situation becomes gravely dangerous. It may be human nature to believe that the worst will never happen. Moreover, the difficulty of predicting a hurricane's exact path seems to encourage some people to gamble with their lives: "It's not going to hit right here. The forecasts have been wrong so many times before."

The American Red Cross identifies another complicating factor: "Eighty to 90 percent of the population now living in hurricane-prone areas have never experienced the core of a 'major' hurricane . . . [but] many of these people have been through weaker storms. The result is a false impression of a hurricane's damage potential."[31]

Lulled by this false impression, some people make a considered decision to ride out the storm so that they can protect their property. Others decide to stay because they just do not think it's going to be as bad as officials predict. They know a

A body surfer in Florida is hit by a mammoth wave generated by an approaching hurricane.

storm may be frightening, but they think they will be safer in their own homes than on the road somewhere. Some people actually view the hurricane as a big adventure: It is quite common, for example, to see surfers playing in the rough surf that precedes a hurricane. They may continue riding the waves long after more cautious people have evacuated the shore.

Whether a person's decision to stay is carefully considered or simply thoughtless, one thing is certain. Anyone who stands in the path of a hurricane is in for a wild ride indeed.

The Hurricane Hits

In a 1993 *National Geographic* article, a survivor of Hurricane Andrew described his experiences during the height of the hurricane: "I heard one window break, so I jumped up and put a mattress against it. But I guess that storm really wanted to get in, 'cause it blew out another window and beat down the front door. Then it knocked down a wall and began suckin' things out. It lifted a mattress off a bed and sucked it up against a window. It was like a vacuum cleaner."[32]

Another survivor recalled his ordeal: "I held the door with my body, but the storm, it was so terrible. Sometimes it seemed it was lifting the walls. It broke the window and tore off the roof. I heard

Survivors of Hurricane Andrew, which demolished this home, describe the experience as terrifying.

someone crying 'Help me, help me.' For three hours . . . it sounded like bombs. It was so terrible . . . the sky was flashing, like when a volcano blows up. I lost everything I have but my life."[33]

Eyewitness hurricane accounts are full of harrowing tales like these. The overriding emotion in such accounts is terror. Clearly, living through a hurricane is one of the most frightening experiences imaginable. From the moment it appears on the horizon until it finally loses power and dies away, a hurricane menaces everyone and everything in its path.

Changing Weather

The first visible sign of an approaching hurricane is unusual wave patterns. In the Gulf of Mexico, for instance, twelve to fifteen waves normally wash up on the shore each minute. When a hurricane is lurking over the horizon, the pattern slows dramatically. Only four or five waves arrive each minute, and they are noticeably larger than usual.

The actual hurricane first shows itself as light, wispy clouds spiking up from the horizon. Called rooster tails, these clouds are made of millions of tiny ice crystals floating in a thin layer high above the storm. According to Gary Jennings, "Early Indian tribes in the Americas recognized these clouds as a portent of the hurricane and taught the first Spanish explorers that the direction from which the clouds fanned was the direction from which the storm would come."[34] The rooster tails may cover the entire sky as the storm draws closer, creating a haze that dims daylight and draws fuzzy halos around the sun and the moon.

Finally the rim of the hurricane itself, called the bar, becomes visible. The approach of the bar can be an awesome sight. According to Jennings, "It appears above the horizon of the sea like a rising mountain of dirty snow—a rounded hump, grayish-white in color. As the hump continues to rise, spreading wider and wider against the sky, its color darkens to gray, then dark gray, then near-black, sometimes tinged with coppery red."[35]

Wind and Rain

Soon after the bar appears, the winds begin to pick up. Because these winds mark the outer tips of the hurricane's spiral bands, they may be strangely gusty. The winds carry the scud—scraps of cloud torn from the hurricane and flung outward before the advancing storm. They may also bring rain.

Below hurricane strength, winds are officially described according to the Beaufort scale, in use since 1858. Force 0 on this scale represents absolutely calm air. A light breeze that is just powerful enough to sway tree branches may be a Force 2 or 3; a strong breeze capable of yanking an umbrella out of a pedestrian's hand might be a Force 6. A gale-force wind of 39 mph measures Force 8. Force 10 describes winds of at least 56 mph, and Force 12 signifies hurricane-strength winds of 75 mph. Wind speeds creep up the Beaufort scale as the center of the storm approaches, and their effect on the surroundings rises correspondingly.

Rain activity also increases as the hurricane nears. At first this activity may be nothing more than quick, scattered showers. But the squalls become more and more violent toward the heart of the storm. As the center of the storm approaches, the wind may carry enough rain at times to fill the air with water. "Visibility was almost non-existent and it was very hard to tell what time of day it was. The color was grayish-black and thick walls of horizontal rain blocked any view,"[36] reports one hurricane survivor.

Violent lightning activity is another characteristic of the outer bands of a hurricane. Thunderstorms scattered throughout the fringe of the storm may spawn thousands of lightning strikes each hour.

A lightning bolt strikes as a hurricane approaches.

Inside the Eyewall

Chaos reigns inside the storm's eyewall. Lightning activity often drops off, but that is small comfort amid winds that spiral inward at full hurricane force, snatching up unsecured objects and flinging them like missiles. Trees bend to the ground; some snap like twigs. Exposed persons may be swept away if the air current is strong enough. In a wind of 150 mph, says Jennings, the laws of physics dictate that a person "would be shoved along the ground—slowly at first, but irresistibly—scraping and grinding, then bouncing and bounding like a tumbleweed."[37]

Rain is propelled horizontally with the wind, as if blasted out of the world's most powerful water cannon. At hurricane speeds, rain becomes a weapon strong enough to destroy buildings and tear the limbs from sturdy trees. But the speed of the water is not the only problem. The sheer quantity of water dumped by the storm (hurricanes unload an average of six to twelve inches of rain at landfall) can lead to flooding and mudslides, which cause devastation of their own.

The intense wind and rain sometimes give birth to other violent weather phenomena, including tornadoes, downbursts (defined as areas where heavy rainfall accelerates air to the ground where it spreads out at speeds greater than 100 mph), and mesoscale vortices (whirling columns of air 150 to 500 feet wide that form at the boundary of the eyewall and eye). Almost all hurricanes spawn at least one tornado or similar phenomenon, and some produce many more. Hurricane Andrew, for example, produced 62 tornadoes. And Hurricane Beulah, which struck southeast Texas in 1967, spawned a record 141 tornadoes.

An Unearthly Noise

As the hurricane rages, the whipping winds generate deafening noise. The sound of the storm is so powerful, and so pervasive, that all other sound is drowned out. Houses collapse in silence. Uprooted trees fly quietly through the air. Thunder, although constant, cannot be heard above the roar of the winds. Even tornadoes, which are so noisy that they are often compared to freight trains, may not be heard.

Hurricane Parties

"Hurricane parties," where groups of people gather to eat, drink, and make merry while the storm passes, are quite common in hurricane-prone areas. Most of the time, everything goes as planned. But partygoers are taking a huge risk. A powerful storm can easily turn a jolly gathering into a massacre. In the book *Storm*, author A. B. C. Whipple describes a 1969 hurricane party that went horribly wrong.

The weather bureau had issued urgent warnings of the approach of Hurricane Camille. The forecasters had labeled it an extremely dangerous storm. . . . Nevertheless, 12 people gathered on the third floor of the Richelieu [Apartments in Pass Christian, Mississippi] to celebrate the coming of Camille. . . . Aside from the 12 partygoers, another dozen people were in the apartment house that evening. At least two of them, Mary Ann Gerlach and her husband, Fritz, were preparing to join the celebrants. "We had been in hurricanes in Florida," she said later. "You get off work and it's—you know—party time."

The Gerlachs never made it to the party. Waves hammered at the picture window in their second-floor living room. "We heard an awful popping sound as the windows went. We held our shoulders to the bedroom door to try to keep the water from coming in. But in about five minutes the bed was floating halfway to the ceiling. You could feel the building swaying like we were in a boat," said Mrs. Gerlach.

Somehow, Mrs. Gerlach managed to swim out a window. She saw her husband disappear beneath the waves. And then, looking back, she watched in horror as the entire Richelieu building collapsed like a child's sand castle into the maelstrom.

The rest of the night was etched in Mrs. Gerlach's memory. She recalled grabbing some wreckage and being driven along by winds so strong that she could scarcely breathe. At last she was deposited in a treetop almost five miles from the beach, and there she stayed until her rescue the following morning.

Of the 24 people in the apartment house, she was the sole survivor. Everyone else had either drowned or been crushed to death when the building crumbled. Mrs. Gerlach supplied their epitaphs when she said: "Whenever there's a hurricane warning now, I get out with all the rest."

Modern hurricane survivors frequently mention not only the monstrous volume but the frightening quality of the noises produced by the storm. This eyewitness account from Hurricane Andrew is typical:

> The electrical explosions across the city grew more intense, yet the fury of the wind swallowed up all sound save the car alarms whining inside the garage. Eventually even the alarms were overwhelmed by the whistling wind. . . . The infamous "hurricane wail" people talk about is in many ways unreal—"the scream of the devil." The piercing sound alone is wicked enough, but mixed with breaking glass and crashing debris, it rattled me inside.[38]

"It sounded like a poltergeist or the devil himself was out there trying to break in," recalled another shaken survivor. "I'll never forget that horrible sound."[39]

Inside the Eye

An area that is hit head-on by a hurricane will experience the passage of the very eye of the storm at some point. The calmness of the eye provides a welcome, though brief, break from the ravages of the eyewall. Inside the eye, the temperature rises. The wind and the rain stop abruptly, as does the unbearable din. After so much noise, the silence of the eye comes as a shock to the ringing ears of the people within.

The pressure in the eye of a major hurricane can be low enough to have noticeable effects on people. "Survivors of some of history's most severe tropical cyclones have spoken of how abrupt changes in barometric pressure made their eardrums pop and their eyes involuntarily fill with tears,"[40] says one scientist. According to another, "The air's abnormally low pressure can . . . burst the tiny blood vessels in the back of the throat, causing a taste of blood in the mouth or a trickle of nosebleed."[41]

If the eye passes during daylight, sunlight may stream down from above. At night the moon and stars may be clearly visible. Also visible at times are thousands of birds that have fled into the eye to escape the hurricane's winds. In the eye they are safe—but they are also trapped. Surrounded by the eyewall, a bird is forced to travel wherever the hurricane chooses to take it. It may be whisked hundreds of miles away from its home before the hurricane finally weakens enough to allow escape. Still, at least the air is calm.

The calmness inside the eye is deceptive, however. Very soon, perhaps within minutes, the far side of the eye will arrive, and the full force of the inner eyewall will slam into the community from the opposite direction. Anyone caught outside when the storm returns is in terrible trouble. But although the danger is generally known, it is quite common for people to venture outside as the eye passes over. Some think the storm has passed; others simply want to look around. Both groups, however, may find that this curiosity is their death sentence, as it was for many during the Miami Beach, Florida, hurricane of 1926. "When winds suddenly stopped roaring, bewildered beachcombers wandered out to the water for a swim or to survey the damage. Forty minutes later, a new wall of wind and water swept over them, drowning more than 100 people,"[42] writes Jeffrey Rosenfeld.

Andrew's winds made projectiles of heavy objects.

Wind Damage

The winds may do even more damage the second time around. Structures that have withstood the hurricane for hours are suddenly smacked full force from the opposite direction as the back side of the storm hits. The reverse strain is too much for many already weakened buildings, and a new round of destruction begins.

Without actually witnessing the storm, it is hard to comprehend just how destructive a hurricane's winds can be. Jay Barnes paints a vivid picture of their power:

> Andrew's winds were strong enough to lift large trucks into the air, shred mobile homes, and hurl massive structural components for blocks. After the storm, planks and pieces of plywood were found impaling the trunks of large palms. . . .

Eighteen-foot-long steel and concrete tie beams with roofs still attached were carried more than 150 feet. Paint was peeled from walls, and street signs were sucked out of the ground and hurled through houses. Flying diesel fuel drums were a hazard, as were signs, awnings, decks, trash barrels,

---

A Scene of Destruction

A powerful hurricane can rip a building to pieces. Bob Blanchard, coauthor with his wife, Melinda, of the book *A Trip to the Beach*, witnessed one such scene on the island of St. Martin during 1998's Hurricane Luis.

The sheets of metal roofing were being peeled off like paper. Pieces of plywood came off next, leaving a skeleton of rafters exposed. The wind rushed into the building. In one swift, sharp move, the roof was ripped apart, rafters and all, and exploded into the air, disappearing into the storm. With the inside of the kitchen now completely exposed, Bob watched as glasses, dishes, pots and pans joined the rest of the building's debris. Now airborne missiles, they smashed into the boats, breaking windows and threatening anything that got in the way. Pieces of wood sheared off lamp posts and snapped palm trees like giant power saws. . . .

Within minutes, the only thing left of what was once a charming little building was a cement block wall that had been the back of the kitchen, and a few pieces of heavy equipment like the range and grill. A stainless steel refrigerator had tipped over on its back and both doors had been ripped off. Inside, bottles of wine were being sucked out and were flying through the air and into the harbor. The refrigerator skidded along the pier like an empty cardboard box, finally tipping over the edge and sinking from sight.

and fence posts that filled the skies. Mobile homes not only blew apart during the storm but disintegrated into aluminum shrapnel that became embedded in surrounding structures.[43]

Storm Surge

Incredibly, a hurricane's winds are not the most destructive aspect of the storm. That distinction belongs to the storm surge—the rise in sea level that accompanies the landfall of a hurricane. Depending on a hurricane's direction of travel, this rise may either precede or trail the eye. Thus, in many cases, the worst truly is yet to come when the eye passes over.

The storm surge is caused mostly by high winds pushing the ocean surface ahead of the hurricane. It typically ranges from a depth of four to five feet in a Category 1 storm to eighteen feet or more in a Category 5 storm. The surge rolls toward land, shoved from behind by the full force of the hurricane. It has been described by hurricane survivors as a rapid rise in water level, as a series of enormous waves, or, worst of all, as a towering wall of water powerful enough to wipe the earth clean of vegetation and structures.

This was the case when Hurricane Hugo arrived in North Carolina. Author William Price Fox describes the scene at one local residence:

> The water was black as ink and coming at them like a moving cliff. . . . The full force of the wave slammed into the house with an impact that rocked it back on its sixteen-foot stilts. The house stayed in that position as the roof peeled back like the lid of a sardine can, and water, sand, seaweed, and fish poured in through the enormous opening. The left side of the house seemed to just fall off. Only the front was standing, completely unsupported. Then the window shattered and collapsed, and the floor beneath them gave way like a trap door.[44]

Such scenes of total destruction are most likely near the coast, where the storm surge is at the peak of its strength. But the surge may roll inland for miles, picking up cars, fallen trees, and any other debris in its path—including people—and whisking it along helplessly. The moving tide inundates homes, tears roadways from their beds, and scours out the foundations of tall buildings, sometimes leading to their collapse.

Inland Flooding

For inland dwellers the intense rainfall that accompanies a hurricane is more worrisome than the storm surge. Slow-moving storms have dumped forty-five inches of rain or more on communities hundreds of miles from the coast. Many people have drowned in the resulting floods. Flooding is, in fact, the deadliest aspect of many hurricanes: "In the last 30 years, inland flooding has been responsible for more than half of the deaths associated with tropical cyclones in the United States,"[45] says a National Hurricane Center spokesman.

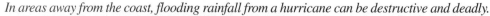

In areas away from the coast, flooding rainfall from a hurricane can be destructive and deadly.

Hurricane Floyd, which brought intense rain and flooding to the eastern United States in 1999, is a case in point. Floyd made landfall as a Category 2 storm near Cape Fear, North Carolina, and traveled up the coast, dumping water as it went. It finally died over New England, but not before causing one of the worst floods in U.S. history. Of the fifty-six human deaths caused by Floyd, fifty were due to drowning. Two million people were forced to evacuate their homes, and damages from flooding alone were estimated at $4.5 billion.

Mudslides

Under certain circumstances the extensive rain brought by a hurricane may also cause mudslides. Mudslides occur when water saturation loosens the soil, especially on steep slopes, and allows it to break free from its underpinnings. The moving earth quickly liquefies and accelerates, reaching speeds over 35 mph. This river of flowing mud can become strong enough to carry large items such as boulders, trees, and cars, and it may be deep enough to bury fields, houses, and people.

One of the worst mudslides in history occurred during Hurricane Mitch in 1998. As the rain poured down, Nicaragua's Casita Volcano filled with water. The pressure mounted. Finally, one of the volcano's walls gave way. A sea of mud and rocks barreled down the mountainside and soon reached populated areas, where it swept away homes—and lives. "I saw an ocean of people crying and trying to enter the sector near the Casita Volcano where dozens of cadavers were floating in the pasture," recalls one survivor. "The thing that made me cry was seeing broken bodies of children and pieces of human bodies partly buried in the mud."[46] Approximately two thousand people were killed in the mudslide, and thousands more were left homeless.

The Storm Departs

A hurricane over land, no matter how powerful it may be, is doomed. There is no way a hurricane can suck the warm fuel it needs from the cold, solid ground. Deprived of its energy source, the storm quickly weakens and eventually falls apart in a final gasp of rain showers.

Under the clearing skies, survivors cautiously poke their heads from their hiding places. If the hurricane was weak, they may find that all is well and that their homes, vehicles, and property have withstood the storm's assault with little or no damage. But the scene may be very different if the hurricane was strong. Floods may continue to rage, property may be destroyed, and lives may be lost. In extreme cases an area may even be flattened by the storm and its aftereffects. Hundreds—perhaps thousands—of people may be left in desperate situations.

But at least the hurricane is over. The winds are gone, the rain has subsided, and the sun shines again. It is finally possible, and safe, for outside agencies to enter the affected area. Relief and rescue efforts can now begin.

The Aftermath

This desperate cry for help was posted to the international community in the wake of 1998's Hurricane Mitch:

> [Honduras] is unraveling as the situation here gets from bad to worse. Basic infrastructure is collapsing, food supplies are running dangerously low, gasoline is being rationed at this time, the relief centers are out of food. . . . The city is cut off by land as all bridges and roads in and out of the city are impassable. The relief flights and air bridge have only one or two days of jet fuel left. The entire country has been devastated by this storm and its aftereffects. . . . Please send help.[47]

This passage points out a terrible truth about hurricanes. The storm itself may come and go within a few hours, but its effects may be felt for years. The immediate need is rescue services for people who have been injured or trapped by the storm. Once those needs are met, the top priority becomes relief—housing, feeding, and clothing people left homeless or helpless by the hurricane. And finally, a community must turn its attention to rebuilding, an effort that may take decades.

None of these tasks is easily achieved. The aftermath of a major hurricane can involve mass disorder and confusion on top of the devastation already wrought by the storm. But it can also bring out the best in people as communities and organizations rally to help those in need.

Agencies Mobilize

The agencies responsible for providing rescue and relief following a hurricane have been mobilized even before the hurricane hits. A major storm will not only injure people and destroy homes; it may also knock out electrical power, contaminate the water supply, shut down hospitals, destroy phone lines, and make the roads impassable for emergency vehicles. People will need shelter, latrines, medicine, food, clean water, and clothing. Supplying all of these necessities is a huge job that requires advance preparation.

In the United States, the Federal Emergency Management Agency (FEMA) is the primary government agency charged with coordinating relief efforts after a disaster, including a hurricane. It is supposed to mobilize when the U.S. president declares a region a federal disaster area, which sometimes occurs even before a hurricane has departed. Immediately after the storm, FEMA is responsible for conducting and coordinating emergency operations to save lives and property by positioning emer-

Hurricane survivors wait to talk with FEMA representatives about receiving assistance.

gency equipment and supplies; evacuating victims; providing food, water, shelter, and medical care to those in need; and restoring critical public services.

As a principal supplier of food, shelter, and emergency medical services to disaster victims, the American Red Cross also plays a crucial role in this effort. In order to respond as quickly as possible, the Red Cross maintains a reserve of material resources—supplies, vehicles, communications equipment, and more—which is, as the agency says, "strategically located around the United States, its territories and possessions, and ready to move into a disaster-affected area at a moment's notice."[48]

The U.S. military also goes on alert. Service personnel in the National Guard and other branches of the armed services participate in relief and rescue activities on an as-needed basis, lending valuable manpower and expertise to the effort.

These organizations, along with the Salvation Army, church groups, ham radio clubs, and other private agencies, track the progress of the hurricane across populated areas. TV and radio transmitters often fail during a hurricane, so relief workers may not know what to expect when they arrive on the scene. But experience has taught them to be prepared for the worst.

Property Damage

A strong hurricane can leave devastation in its wake. The city of Homestead, Florida, which bore the brunt of Hurricane Andrew's force, is a testament to this statement. "Homestead looked as if it had been hit by the blast of a nuclear explosion. Everywhere we looked we saw mass destruction,"[49] wrote one observer. The residential portion of the town was "razed almost beyond recognition,"[50] said another observer, and nearby Homestead Air Force Base was flattened.

Marinas, exposed as they are to the sea, may be shredded by the hurricane. Such was the case during Hurricane Luis, which crushed the Leeward Islands in the West Indies in 1998. Hundreds of boats had taken refuge in the harbor of St. Martin, hoping to ride out the storm in safety. But that hope was dashed by Luis's

A Scene of Chaos

Hurricane Andrew's aftermath was a scene of near anarchy. In his article "Hurricane's Fury Left 165 Square Miles Pounded into the Ground," reporter William Booth of the *Washington Post* describes the confusion.

The hurricane continues to imbue South Florida with an end-of-the-world aura. Television anchors appear on the screen unshaven and disheveled. Suburban housewives bathe in man-made lakes. Turnpike toll booths are abandoned. Confused old men walk into field hospitals barefoot. . . .

Because many people in the devastated areas had no radios or batteries, the location of food distribution sites has been a mystery. Even when they knew where to get free food, many lacked cars or the gasoline to get there. Each time word spread about establishment of a new relief outlet, people suddenly would swarm forward on foot, and National Guard troops often had to be summoned to keep order. . . .

Throughout the area, residents spray-painted what remained standing of the fronts of their houses with the names of their insurers, the house address and the insurance policy number because street signs and mailboxes were nonexistent. Even directing visitors by citing landmarks, such as turn left at the 7-Eleven, became useless because the 7-Eleven often had ceased to exist. . . .

There has been widespread looting and price gouging, as thieves worked to take advantage of a general feeling of lawlessness. . . . At night, in darkened streets cordoned by National Guard troops enforcing a curfew, machine-gun fire has been heard. Spray-painted on the side of a house . . . was: "I'm armed and dangerous! Looters shot on sight!"

"Everyone is armed, everyone is walking around with guns," said Navy physician Sharon Wood. . . . Senior citizens sleep at night with revolvers by their sides.

Lawlessness compounded the chaos after Hurricane Andrew.

150-mph winds. "Sunken boats were everywhere. An unimaginable number of masts stuck up out of the water. Down in the far corner [of the marina], a pile of boats lay entangled and destroyed beyond belief. Hundreds of motor yachts, sailboats and barges were heaped on top of each other in a tangle of ropes, masts, broken glass, hulls, sterns and keels,"[51] wrote survivors of the storm.

Property damage can also cause some unusual crises. One such crisis occurred during Hurricane Andrew, when thousands of animals escaped from Florida zoos and research facilities. More than 450 primates, including 50 to 100 large and potentially dangerous baboons, overran Dade County. About 1,000 exotic birds flew free, never to be recovered. Hundreds of poisonous reptiles slithered away from captivity. And although Miami's Metrozoo held fast, rumors of escaped lions and panthers further terrorized an already traumatized population.

The Environmental Toll

But property damage, no matter how extreme, often pales in comparison to the environmental damage wrought by a hurricane. In 1989 Hurricane Hugo destroyed an estimated 6 billion board feet of timber in South Carolina, setting the state's lumber industry back decades. Hurricane Fran, which decimated North Carolina in 1996, took an especially heavy toll on coastal property, as historian Jay Barnes notes: "The tide was so powerful . . . that it carved six new inlets across Topsail Island, slicing up the beach road and isolating entire communities. . . . Heavy beach erosion had moved mountains of sand, wiping out what remained of the dunes and their fragile vegetation. So much construction debris, paper, plastic, glass, appliances, and toxic household products was washed into the marsh or buried in the sand that the area might never be completely cleaned up."[52] A storm surge of this magnitude may also saturate farmland with ocean salt, rendering it unusable for years to come.

Regular flooding can have unexpectedly dire consequences, as it did following Hurricane Floyd. Before the storm North Carolina was home to 9 million hogs. The flooding not only drowned untold numbers of these animals, it also released millions of gallons of untreated hog manure into the environment. "Pools of rank,

Protecting what remains of a family's property after a destructive hurricane can be an added burden.

fetid water topped with rainbow slicks stood everywhere, and roadside ditches were filled with the vile brew. A hideous stench hung over the county—a combination of raw sewage, animal waste, petrochemicals, pesticides, and rotting carcasses,"[53] wrote one reporter in the aftermath of the storm. Scientists estimate that the toxins released by Floyd's floods may contaminate the area's groundwater for as much as forty years.

The Human Toll

The human toll can be equally appalling, particularly in areas with long, shallow coastal shelves. This geography amplifies the storm surge, which may become deep enough and powerful enough to drown scores of people.

The greatest death toll in U.S. hurricane history was due to precisely this effect. Storm waters flooded the town of Galveston, Texas, during the Great Galveston Hurricane of 1900. At least

6,500 and perhaps as many as 12,000 lives were lost in the deluge; when the waters receded, the streets were paved with the bodies of the dead. One author describes the grisly scene: "All that remained of thousands of homes and many of the people who had lived in them was a great mound of wreckage jammed with bodies. . . . Galveston Bay was clogged with human bodies. . . . Many bodies were naked or near-naked, their clothes ripped off by protruding nails, jagged pieces of wood, broken glass, and flying debris."[54]

The Galveston tragedy, however, is eclipsed by the losses due to other disastrous storms around the world. Geography has been particularly unkind to Bangladesh, which sits at the northern end of the shallow Bay of Bengal. The narrowing bay funnels the storm surge into an ever-smaller area, making it both deeper and

United States Hurricanes Causing 100+ Deaths, 1900–2000

Hurricane*	Year	Category	Deaths**
Great Galveston Hurricane (TX)	1900	4	8000+
Lake Okeechobee (FL)	1928	4	1836
Florida Keys/South Texas	1919	4	600
New England	1938	3	600
Florida Keys	1935	5	408
Audrey (LA/TX)	1957	4	390
Northeast U.S.	1944	3	390
Grand Isle (LA)	1909	4	350
New Orleans (LA)	1915	4	275
Galveston (TX)	1915	4	275
Camille (MS/LA)	1969	5	256
Florida/Mississippi/Alabama	1926	4	243
Diane (northeast U.S.)	1955	1	184
Southeast Florida	1906	2	164
Mississippi/Alabama/Pensacola, FL	1906	3	134
Agnes (northeast U.S.)	1972	1	122

Locations are given if a hurricane was unnamed.

**Some numbers are approximate*

Source: Landsea FAQ, www.aoml.noaa.gov/hrd/tcfaq/tcfaqE.html

more powerful. By the time the surge reaches land, it packs enough punch to roll miles inland, destroying everything in its path. As many as 500,000 people lost their lives during the Bangladesh Cyclone of 1970, the deadliest hurricane in recorded history, and 139,000 people drowned during a cyclone that hit the area in 1991.

Rescue Efforts

Despite a hurricane's deadly potential, relatively few people are killed during most storms in North America. Many, however, are left in dire straits after the storm's passage. People washed away by the storm surge are sometimes found clinging to tree branches and to the roofs of floating houses. Others are pinned inside their homes when the walls collapse. Still others may have been badly injured by flying debris or trapped in mudslides.

Rescue efforts following a hurricane include helping stranded pets.

Emergency rescue efforts swing into action immediately following the storm. Both civilian forces and the military play major roles in these efforts. Local fire departments and the National Guard scour the wreckage, plucking survivors from the debris and whisking them to temporary medical facilities manned by FEMA and the Red Cross. Other military agencies, including the Coast Guard and Army Airborne units, deploy rescue helicopters to affected areas.

Helicopters are particularly useful in flooded areas that land-based vehicles cannot reach. They saved countless lives, for example, in the watery aftermath of Hurricane Floyd. An airport official describes the scene:

Hurricane victims often must rely on supplies provided by relief agencies.

[Helicopters rescued] thousands of hurricane victims stranded on roof tops, from trees, cars and trucks, and flooded areas in eastern North Carolina. Flying hundreds of missions, not only did they pick up people, they airlifted horses, cattle, and many dogs to safety. The sounds of the helicopters chopping back and forth in the skies all over eastern NC have certainly made up the sound track for the drama that has unfolded over the past week.[55]

Disaster Relief

While the rescuers do their work, trucks full of food, clothing, water, medical supplies, and other crucial items rumble into affected areas. Approximately twenty-five federally appointed relief organizations quickly set up tent headquarters from which they will supply hurricane survivors with the basic necessities of life. Many private groups and concerned citizens voluntarily join the effort, sometimes driving hundreds of miles to reach the scene.

Utility crews also swing into action, working around the clock to fix downed power and telephone lines, restore the area's water supply, and replace stop lights and street signs. Sanitation vehicles remove trees, branches, palm fronds, seaweed, and any other debris clogging the streets, and road crews patch damaged pavement as best they can.

These services are extremely helpful in the days and weeks immediately following the hurricane. But they are only temporary fixes. After their emergency survival needs are met, many storm victims will need longer-term help. One of FEMA's most important functions is helping disaster victims to file for federal financial assistance. The Red Cross provides counseling to traumatized survivors and sponsors educational programs to prepare the community for future disasters. And private operators, such as roofers, construction crews, electricians, and plumbers, may have their hands full for years as they work to restore form and function to structures that have been damaged by the storm.

The recovery period can bring out the best in people. In his 1993 State of the State Address, then Florida governor Lawton Chiles commented on this phenomenon: "In the aftermath of Andrew, courageous acts were the order of the day. Countless people reached outside their own problems to help others. Through all of the sadness, we saw people helping people regardless of race, religion or station in life. Rows of houses became neighborhoods; strangers became friends. . . . In short, crowds became communities."[56]

Unfortunately, there is a flip side to this bright coin. Andrew's aftermath also brought confusion and lawlessness. "The really bad side of some people came out," observed then Homestead mayor Tad DeMilly. "Those were mostly people who came in to loot . . . [but] we couldn't arrest looters because we had nowhere to put them. It was verging on anarchy."[57]

An Emotional Crisis

A hurricane's effects cannot be measured solely in dollars. Hurricanes also have lasting psychological impacts. Some psychologists estimate that up to 80 percent of the survivors of a major hurricane will suffer from post-traumatic stress for at least a year, and 5 to 10 percent will experience a more serious mental disorder. For this reason, crisis counseling is now a standard part of hurricane relief operations in the United States.

In *The Hurricane Handbook*, authors Sharon Maddux Carpenter and Toni Garcia Carpenter describe some of the feelings that survivors typically experience.

The "need to know something" is an immediate response of persons during and immediately after a hurricane. People crave information about the extent of the destruction, the welfare of loved ones, and where to go for help and necessary supplies.

After the disbelief of the first few days following a hurricane, reality emerges. Survivors begin to understand how difficult it will be to reestablish their "pre-Hurricane" lives. Many survivors realize that they will need to begin again. The loss of so many possessions is very difficult. While trying to survive from day-to-day is the primary priority, many adults experience an increasing sense of anger, helplessness, and depression. Some people who suffer little damage become quiet and withdrawn. In some cases, they are trying to understand how to deal with their guilt at having been spared.

Experiencing such a strong natural disaster as a hurricane changes your surroundings and your life forever. It takes time to adjust to the new realities, to grieve for familiar people, places, and items that have been lost. Counseling services will be available and may be a very important part of your own, personal recovery. Don't hesitate to make use of them.

Living through a hurricane can be an emotional, life-changing experience.

A Troubled History

The general relief effort, too, has historically drawn criticism. Hurricane survivors have often complained that the government's typical disaster response is too little, too late. But not much was done about these complaints until Andrew thrust the inefficiencies of federal disaster-management agencies into the spotlight. "Where in the hell is the cavalry?" demanded an angry Kate Hale, director of Dade County's Office of Emergency Management, when promised assistance had not yet appeared several days after the passage of the storm. "We need food. We need water. We need people. For God's sake, where are they?"[58]

Although relief agencies on the scene eventually did a great deal of good, observers and participants felt that the response was woefully disorganized, particularly in the days immediately following the storm. FEMA itself later admitted that "the overall federal response, as well as the Florida response, was uncoordinated, confused, and often inadequate."[59]

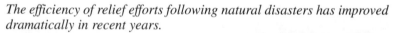

The efficiency of relief efforts following natural disasters has improved dramatically in recent years.

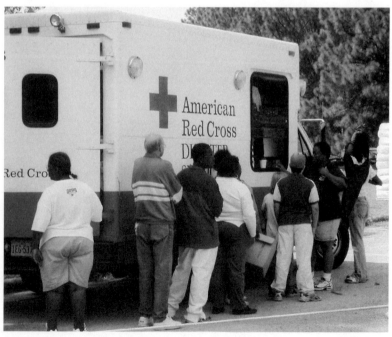

In this regard, however, Andrew's legacy has been positive. In response to the criticism, federal and state agencies launched comprehensive studies of their emergency management systems, looking for ways to improve response times and effectiveness. "We have changed the way we do emergency management to be more effective and more efficient . . . and to be there when we're needed most, directly before and after disaster. And we have streamlined our recovery process so that communities can rebuild faster and more safely,"[60] said FEMA director James Witt in 1996, just four years after Andrew made landfall.

People still complain—"Federal and state government reactions ended up disrupting far more lives than were seriously threatened by the hurricane itself,"[61] griped one writer following Hurricane Floyd—but most agree that the hurricane response and relief system today is vastly more effective than it was just a decade ago.

Cleaning up and rebuilding a community ravaged by a hurricane is an enormous task.

Rebuilding

Even the best rescue and relief effort, however, is only a short-term solution. Once the crisis is past, a hurricane-ravaged community must face the larger task of rebuilding businesses, homes, and other structures that were damaged or destroyed by the storm. The effort moves slowly, in part because of a labor shortage: In many cases, there simply are too few qualified contractors to do so much work quickly. Homeowners are forced to place their lives on hold, sometimes for months, while they wait for help to become available.

The shortage of skilled labor leads to another common problem. Smelling easy money, hordes of unskilled or unscrupulous contractors descend on storm-weary populations. People desperate to repair or rebuild their homes may hand over their money without bothering to check a contractor's credentials. The result is often poor workmanship—or in some cases, no work at all. A writer for a national magazine reports that in Andrew's aftermath, "People without scruples made out like bandits at the expense of people who had lost the roofs over their heads. Money changed hands, but the promised work was not always done or was done poorly."[62]

Most communities eventually overcome these problems and are more or less restored to their former selves in the years following a hurricane. But sometimes the job of rebuilding is so immense that it may never be completed. In some cases area residents simply lack the expertise and experience to tackle the job. "Those folks wouldn't know a [rebuilding] plan if it walked up and said 'I'm a plan,'"[63] grumbled one economic development consultant in reference to a small North Carolina town struggling to rebuild after Hurricane Floyd. In other cases the damage is simply so overwhelming that residents move from the area, never to return. Homestead, for example, has never fully recovered from Andrew's impact. Once a thriving community, the town today is a shadow of its former self.

The Expense Mounts

The rebuilding effort is not only difficult but expensive, sometimes astonishingly so. Damages from Hurricane Andrew, the costliest hurricane in U.S. history, exceeded $26.5 billion. Hurricane Hugo was the nation's second-costliest storm, racking up $7 billion in destruction. Floyd's total hovered around $6 billion, and Hurricane Georges of 1998 did an estimated $5.8 billion worth of damage.

Costs associated with Hurricane Andrew were high enough to drive eight insurance companies out of business. Another twenty-three companies announced plans to pull out of the Florida market and other hurricane-prone areas, including Louisiana and Hawaii. A lawyer for one large insurance company spoke for the industry when he commented that another storm like Andrew "could wipe us out. . . . It's irresponsible

Volunteers clean a church building after a hurricane. The costs associated with hurricanes are immense.

to continue to insure more homes than we can afford to pay claims for."[64]

The insurance companies have reason to worry. Andrew was devastating enough as it was—but had it hit just a few miles north, it would have traveled directly over the heavily developed city of Miami, perhaps doubling or tripling the damage. And scientists say that it is only a matter of time before a monster hurricane does make landfall in a highly populated area. "The Big One" might come this year, it might come next year, or it might not come for decades. But the laws of statistics say that it *is* coming.

Taming the Winds

"No one knows when or where [a catastrophic hurricane] will strike, but we do know that eventually it will blast ashore somewhere and cause massive destruction. . . . Since there is nothing anyone can do to alter that foreboding reality, the question is: Are we ready for the next great hurricane?"[65]

Hurricane historian Jay Barnes bluntly expresses a fear that has plagued scientists and governments for decades. History has demonstrated again and again the terrible toll that a major hurricane can take on a densely populated area. A killer storm is therefore the nightmare of every disaster-management official—and this is one nightmare that is all too likely to come true someday.

Until relatively recently there was little anyone could do about the so-called hurricane problem. The technological advances of the past sixty years or so, however, have made it possible for humankind to wage a crusade against nature, with mixed results. Efforts to destroy hurricanes have met with utter failure. Tracking efforts, on the other hand, have been much more successful; thousands of lives have doubtlessly been saved through increased warning times. And moving forward, efforts to promote preparedness may prove to be the best strategy of all.

The push to promote hurricane readiness is an ongoing project. It is not yet possible to predict whether residents and agencies will, indeed, be prepared for the next great hurricane. But if the past is any indication, the effort will be interesting to watch.

Seeding the Storm

The war against hurricanes started with a simple scientific principle. In 1946 scientist Vincent Schaefer discovered that it was possible to create rain by "seeding" clouds with dry ice or silver iodide crystals. This idea immediately captured the imagination of the U.S. government. Would it be possible to "seed" hurricanes at sea, causing them to dump most or all of their moisture before they reached land? In 1947 several agencies collaborated in launching Project Cirrus, a hurricane-seeding experiment that they hoped would answer this question.

Project Cirrus's big moment came on October 13, 1947, when an unnamed Category 2 hurricane came within striking distance of the coast of northern Florida. An airplane flew over

Project Cirrus leader Vincent Schaefer tries to turn his breath into crystals as part of his cloud-seeding research in the 1940s.

the hurricane, sprinkling approximately eighty pounds of dry ice over the system. Observers inside the airplane noticed that the clouds looked different immediately after the seeding, but there was no apparent change in the storm's strength or structure. Disappointed with the results of the experiment, the researchers headed home, hoping to try again another day.

But soon after the seeding, the hurricane abruptly changed its course. It made landfall in Georgia and traveled up the coast to North Carolina, battering homes and dumping rain as it went. Although no lives were lost, furious residents blamed Project Cirrus for their misery. The blame probably was not warranted. As science writer Patrick Fitzpatrick points out, "It is extremely unlikely the seeding altered the course, because hurricanes are mostly guided by constantly shifting large-scale atmospheric currents."[66] But public opinion was strong, and Project Cirrus ground to a halt.

Project Stormfury

Project Stormfury was the federal government's next major offensive. Active from 1961 through 1983, Stormfury was also based on the seeding principle. But by this time scientists had more specific ideas about how to accomplish their goals. Years of observation had educated the scientific community about the basic structure of hurricanes. They understood that the lower the pressure in the eye, the more powerful the storm. Experience had also taught them that a smaller eye usually meant lower pressure. Therefore, they reasoned, why not seed *only* the eyewall? The resulting instability would cause the eyewall to collapse. When it re-formed, scientists hypothesized, its diameter would be greater, and the storm's power would accordingly be reduced.

Although this method seemed to produce some good results, the effects were disappointingly brief. In 1961 eyewall seeding reduced sustained winds in Hurricane Esther from 130 mph to 119 mph, but the storm bounced back to its original strength within two hours. In 1967 Hurricane Beulah dropped from 89 mph to 80 mph under Stormfury's assault. But this change, too, was temporary.

Did Project Stormfury Work?

One of the great debates in hurricane history is whether Project Stormfury actually achieved the results it claimed, or whether observed changes in seeded storms were just a coincidence. In his *Omni* magazine article "Hurricanes: Reaping the Whirlwind," author Carl Posey explains both sides of the issue.

Flights into 1980's Hurricane Allen . . . revealed precisely the kind of wind variations that Stormfury scientists had measured in Debbie after seeding. The intended effect of seeding, it was suddenly apparent, happened all the time, naturally.

Such news meant different things to different scientists, depending on whether they were Stormfury believers or infidels. To the latter, the results from Allen proved that the changes seen in a seeded Debbie—and in the earlier storms as well—were merely an illusion of human intervention, a natural coincidence. To believers, the evidence points just the other way. The variations seen in Allen show that the structural changes Stormfury hoped to achieve are inherent in hurricane behavior, ready to be triggered by some human agent.

Robert Sheets, director of the National Hurricane Center in Coral Gables, Florida, directed Stormfury during the 1970s and until its demise early in the 1980s. A scientist who has spent a long research career flying around inside hurricanes, Sheets remains a true believer. "I was converted by the Debbie results," he says. He himself analyzed the data, and it convinced him that the hypothesis is correct. "What we can't verify is that we caused the change," he says. "The magnitude of the system sort of overwhelms what can and cannot be done."

Project Stormfury's most successful seeding was done on Hurricane Debbie in 1969. More than a thousand pounds of silver iodide were dumped into Debbie's eyewall, with the apparent result that sustained winds dropped from 100 mph to 70 mph. Within a day, however, Debbie's winds were up to 125 mph. A second seeding, this time with two thousand pounds of silver iodide, dropped the winds to 110 mph. But Debbie once again recovered from the blow, regaining her original strength within hours.

Despite these successes, the project's original goals were not being met. Hurricanes were just as dangerous as ever. Many scientists also questioned whether Stormfury's seeding had done anything at all. The diminished strength of seeded storms might have occurred even without Stormfury's intervention, they argued. Inconclusive results and political criticism mounted until Project Stormfury was finally canceled in 1983.

A Series of Solutions

But the hurricane problem remained. In Stormfury's wake, a flurry of proposed solutions emerged.

The most popular theory involved detonating nuclear weapons in the heart of the storm. Some scientists believed that the explosions would disrupt the hurricane and make it fall apart. But these scientists failed to appreciate the full power of the storm. The heat energy released by a hurricane is approximately equal to a ten-megaton bomb exploding every twenty minutes. In the colorful words of one scientist, halting a hurricane with a nuclear bomb "seems more futile than trying to stop a charging elephant by throwing a ping-pong ball at it."[67] The nuclear-bomb theory had another big problem: The hurricane's winds would scatter the deadly radiation released by the explosion for hundreds of miles, possibly endangering millions of people.

Other hurricane-prevention theories focused on cutting off the storm's heat source. Scientists variously suggested towing icebergs from the Arctic to chill the waters in the hurricane's path, covering the ocean with a thin layer of liquid that would retard evaporation, and dumping huge quantities of dark powder into the atmosphere to suck up the hurricane's heat. But none of these ideas was practical, and none was ever tested.

Years of failure finally killed all efforts to control hurricanes. Today, it is generally accepted that hurricanes are a fact of life. The American Meteorological Society took a firm stand on this subject in 1998 in its policy statement on planned and inadvertent weather modification, stating, "There is no sound physical hypothesis for the modification of hurricanes, tornadoes, or damaging winds in general."[68] The Atlantic Oceanographic and Meteorological Laboratory (AOML), echoing the view that there is no certain route to the elimination of hurricane danger, reports that "No federal agencies are presently doing or planning research on hurricane modification."[69]

A Successful Prediction Strategist

Because hurricanes cannot be stopped, scientists are working instead to improve their prediction techniques. William Gray of Colorado State University's Department of Atmospheric Science is the best-known authority in this field. In June of each year Gray predicts the number of named storms, hurricanes, and intense hurricanes that will occur during the upcoming Atlantic storm season. He then updates his predictions in August to take current weather patterns into account. Gray bases his predictions on a number of global weather factors, including fluctuating ocean temperatures, west African rainfall totals, high-level wind patterns, and many others.

Dr. William Gray predicts a big increase in the number of Atlantic hurricanes.

Over eighteen years, Gray has proved his ability to predict whether a hurricane season will be light or heavy. For this reason, his yearly forecasts are always much anticipated and highly publicized. Gray is rarely *exactly* correct, but he almost always comes close.

This spells bad news for the Atlantic basin, because Gray's current forecast calls for greatly increased hurricane activity in the near future. The past few decades have been unusually quiet, he says—but this trend is unlikely to continue. "Climatology will eventually right itself, and we must expect a great increase in landfalling major hurricanes in the coming decades," stated Gray in his 2001 forecast. "We should see levels of hurricane damage never before experienced."[70]

Improved Tracking Models

This frightening possibility has increased pressure on the National Hurricane Center to improve its hurricane tracking models. Better forecasts will not stop the storm from coming, but they may give people time to get out of its way.

Building a better forecast is a tough job. As one author points out, "Years of study into the tracking of cyclonic storms has yet to result in an accurate prediction beyond 24 hours of landfall." As a result, "Entire sections of coastline can either be needlessly evacuated or left vulnerable as a powerful hurricane, defying the favored forecast, makes a surprise landfall."[71] Despite the challenges, however, hurricane prediction techniques have slowly improved over the last few decades. The AOML estimates that "over the last 30 years, the decrease in forecast error has averaged about 1% per year, largely because of improved computer models."[72]

The yearly gain sounds small, but the grand total of approximately 30 percent represents a major advance in hurricane tracking and prediction techniques. Today the NHC is able to post hurricane warnings with greater accuracy than at any other time in history. People in threatened areas are better able to prepare their homes and evacuate as a result of these improved warnings.

Getting the Word Out

Warnings today are not only more accurate than they were thirty years ago; they are also distributed much more widely and promptly thanks to TV, radio, and other media outlets. The NHC has carefully nurtured its relationship with broadcasters, to the

The Cost of a Warning

Raising a hurricane warning is expensive. "When Hurricanes Collide," a radio show produced by the Earth and Sky Radio Series, explains just how expensive.

The estimated cost of a hurricane warning can be half a million to a million dollars per mile of coastline affected. This figure includes not only the preparation work to protect homes and other buildings and the cost of moving airplanes and boats to other locations, but also the cost to the economy of lost productivity and canceled vacations.

Meanwhile, the typical hurricane affects an area of land about 100 miles wide. To be prudent, a hurricane forecaster will allow for a hundred-mile margin on each side of what seems to be the hurricane's main path. So you can see that the cost to evacuate 300 miles of coastline can be quite high.

Reducing this cost is a major goal of the current effort to improve hurricane prediction models. The National Oceanographic and Atmospheric Administration's strategic plan argues that increased funding for improved tracking will be more than offset by savings in property damage.

An average hurricane today . . . involves preparation and evacuation costs to the public in excess of $50 million per event. Improved predictions of hurricane tracks . . . will reduce the size of the warning areas, saving more than $5 million per storm. This is more than 50 times the cost of the proposed additional observations. . . . The enhanced observations [will also] result in earlier, more accurate warnings. This additional preparation time will allow the public to protect residences better and relocate boats, recreational vehicles, etc., to safe locations. Such actions would save property owners and insurance companies several billion dollars over the course of a decade.

point of allowing news crews to transmit directly from the center during times of crisis. Top NHC officials also make themselves available for interviews when a storm approaches, thus ensuring that accurate information is issued to the public.

FEMA and the Red Cross also work to prepare the public for coming storms. But unlike the NHC, which responds only to immediate threats, these agencies mount year-round disaster preparedness campaigns. Red Cross efforts fall mostly in the area of education. The organization provides brochures, classes, and other services that teach residents of hurricane-prone areas what to do when a storm threatens. FEMA's efforts are broader in scope. In addition to educational services, FEMA works to promote better building design and construction practices, shift homes and businesses away from high-risk areas, and assist local officials with effective community planning. The organization also provides grants for activities that may reduce the risk of future hurricane damage. These mitigation efforts, as they are called, are long-term programs and have no immediate goal. But over time, it is hoped, they will save countless lives.

Getting Ready

Communities that have endured a hurricane take mitigation efforts very seriously. The city of Galveston, for example, erected a sturdy seawall following the disastrous hurricane of 1900. The building effort paid off just fifteen years later when a similar hurricane hit the city. The brand-new seawall shielded Galveston from the worst effects of the storm surge that accompanied the hurricane, with the result that only eight lives were lost. Today the city's Emergency Management Division continues to protect Galveston through contingency planning, education, facility upgrades, and other services.

Miami, too, is getting ready for the next big one. In Andrew's wake, the local government passed tougher building codes and stricter enforcement laws in the hope of "hurricane-proofing" the city. Miami officials have also worked to forge stronger bonds with agencies that will be involved in any future disaster mobilization. Better communication, they hope, will mean a smoother response when the time comes.

Communities that have weathered a hurricane understand the importance of planning and preparation.

Major mitigation efforts, unfortunately, are not the norm. Many people who have never lived through a devastating hurricane fail to take the need to prepare seriously. Longtime residents of coastal communities do nothing to get ready for the inevitable blow—"Every storm that's come here has missed us,"[73] shrugged one Florida resident—and former inlanders blithely build new homes in vulnerable areas. "We're seeing more and more people and structures in places where you get really bad storms,"[74] commented one scientist. An insurance industry analyst observed the same phenomenon, noting that greater numbers of people are moving to the coast. "I can't fathom how people can take such risks,"[75] she added.

Population Issues

Yet millions do take such risks. The National Weather Service (NWS) estimates that 45 million permanent residents live along

A dramatic increase in coastal populations, swelled further by vacationers, has created a potentially dangerous situation on U.S. coastlines.

hurricane-prone coastlines, and that number is growing. But the permanent residents are not the only issue. During weekends, holidays, and vacations, the coastal population may swell to dozens of times its original size as visitors flock to the sunny seashore. The result of all this coastal congestion, says the NWS, is that "the United States has a significant hurricane problem."[76]

The problem is twofold. The first and most obvious issue is the increased destruction a hurricane might cause. "From Maine to Texas, our coastline is filled with new homes, condominium towers, and cities built on sand, waiting for the next storm to threaten its residents and their dreams,"[77] notes the NWS. In all of history no other civilization has ever presented Mother Nature with such a substantial target. Some analysts feel that a major hurricane could do enough damage in certain areas to severely harm the U.S. economy.

The second issue is less obvious than the financial one, but more worrisome. The construction of new roadways has not kept pace with coastal population growth. It is seldom possible to post a hurricane warning more than twenty-four hours in advance, but planning officials estimate that it will take eighty hours or more to evacuate some communities. Simple math dictates that a complete evacuation would be impossible if a hurricane were to strike such an area. The loss of human life in this situation could exceed anything ever seen in the United States.

Hurricane Activity Is Increasing

Most of the U.S. coastal building boom has occurred in recent decades, roughly coinciding with a quiet Atlantic hurricane period that stretched from 1970 through the mid-1990s. During this period hurricane activity was greatly reduced from what it had been in the busy 1950s and 1960s, probably because of cooler-than-usual waters in the North Atlantic. But the relatively quiet phase seems to have come to an end.

Some scientists have blamed the recent increase in hurricane activity on global warming. They reason that a rise in the temperature of ocean waters will naturally lead to more and stronger hurricanes. But other scientists disagree with the global warming hypothesis, William Gray among them. "[Global warming] is a very slow and gradual process that might only be expected to bring about small changes in global circulation over periods of 50 to 100 years. It could not cause the abrupt and dramatic upturn in hurricane activity as occurred between 1994 and 1995,"[78] he argues.

Gray also points out that although Atlantic hurricane activity has picked up in recent years, worldwide hurricane activity actually decreased between 1995 and 2000. If global warming is causing a rise in storm activity, it should do so uniformly. Because this has not happened, Gray feels that global warming probably is not the culprit. Long-term global weather fluctuations, he says, are a more logical cause. According to Gray and many others, it is likely that Atlantic hurricane activity alternates between active and quiet phases lasting twenty-five to forty years each. Recent busy years may simply indicate that our quiet time is up.

What the Future Holds

For whatever reason, Atlantic hurricane activity does appear to be on the rise. Coupled with the ever-increasing coastal population of the United States, this increased activity may one day cause a disaster of epic proportions. A major hurricane that scored a direct hit on New York City's Manhattan Island, for example, would cause death and destruction on a scale that is impossible to comprehend.

Tragedy will strike in other parts of the world, too. Bangladesh, which has already sacrificed millions to Hurican, will undoubtedly be struck again. So will the Leeward Islands, the West Indies, Central America, India, Indonesia, northern Australia, and other vulnerable areas around the globe. Countries that are too poor to prepare for the inevitable will be hit especially hard, and their miseries will be added to the long record of human suffering.

But there is a positive note in the long-term hurricane outlook. Improved technology is enabling scientists to learn more and more about how hurricanes form and how they travel. This knowledge in turn improves preparedness efforts. And every time a hurricane does strike land, people learn a little bit more about bracing for and coping with these monster storms. Modern communications allow these lessons to be shared around the world in the blink of an eye, which means that a city in Costa Rica can benefit from the experiences of a village in Burma.

It is unlikely that mankind will ever be able to control hurricanes. But today, for the first time in history, tools are available to help people live with hurricanes instead of die with them.

Notes

Introduction: A History of Destruction

1. Quoted in Patrick J. Fitzpatrick, *Natural Disasters: Hurricanes*. Santa Barbara, CA: ABC-CLIO, 1999, pp. 153–54.

2. Quoted in Lyall Watson, *Heaven's Breath: A Natural History of the Wind*. New York: William Morrow, 1984, p. 251.

Chapter 1: A Storm Is Born

3. Roger A. Pielke, *The Hurricane*. London: Routledge, 1990, p. 32.

4. Pielke, *The Hurricane*, p. 3.

5. David E. Fisher, *The Scariest Place on Earth: Eye to Eye with Hurricanes*. New York: Random House, 1994, p. 25.

6. Jeffrey Rosenfeld, *Eye of the Storm: Inside the World's Deadliest Hurricanes, Tornadoes, and Blizzards*. New York: Plenum Trade, 1999, p. 244.

7. Fitzpatrick, *Natural Disasters: Hurricanes*, pp. 6–7.

8. Fisher, *The Scariest Place on Earth*, p. 45.

9. Fitzpatrick, *Natural Disasters: Hurricanes*, p. 13.

10. Quoted in Pielke, *The Hurricane*, p. 40.

11. Gary Jennings, *The Killer Storms: Hurricanes, Typhoons, and Tornadoes*. Philadelphia: J. B. Lippincott, 1970, p. 59.

Chapter 2: Storm Watch

12. Fatty Goodlander, "How to Prepare Your Vessel to Survive a Hurricane in the U.S. Virgin Islands," Virgin Islands Territorial Emergency Management Agency (VITEMA) publication, 1998, p. 5.

13. Rosenfeld, *Eye of the Storm*, pp. 236–37.

14. Quoted in Rosenfeld, *Eye of the Storm*, p. 237.

15. Christopher W. Landsea, "Frequently Asked Questions: Hurricanes, Typhoons, and Tropical Cyclones," www.aoml.noaa.gov/hrd/tcfaq/tcfaqD.html.

16. Fitzpatrick, *Natural Disasters: Hurricanes*, pp. 26–27.

17. Fisher, *The Scariest Place on Earth*, pp. 79–80.

18. Fisher, *The Scariest Place on Earth*, pp. 81–82.

19. Rosenfeld, *Eye of the Storm*, p. 255.

20. Rosenfeld, *Eye of the Storm*, p. 255.

Chapter 3: The Hurricane Approaches

21. David Hancock and Anthony Faiola, "Bigger, Stronger, Closer," *Miami Herald*, August 23, 1992. NewsLibrary, www.newslibrary.com.

22. Quoted in Hancock and Faiola, "Bigger, Stronger, Closer."

23. David Longshore, *Encyclopedia of Hurricanes, Typhoons, and Cyclones*. New York: Facts On File, 1998, p. 233.

24. United States Air Force Reserve Weather Reconnaissance Fact Sheet, www.hurricanehunters.com/facrec.htm.

25. Fisher, *The Scariest Place on Earth,* p. 84

26. Landsea, "Frequently Asked Questions."

27. American Red Cross website, "Hurricane," www.redcross.org/disaster/safety/guide/hurricane.html

28. Jay Barnes, *Florida's Hurricane History*. Chapel Hill: University of North Carolina Press, 1998, pp. 305–306.

29. *South Florida Sun-Sentinel,* "Finding Shelter for Your Family," posted on Newsday.com, cnews.tribune.com/news/story/0,1162,newsday-storm-64343,00.html.

30. William Price Fox, *Lunatic Wind: Surviving the Storm of the Century*. Chapel Hill, NC: Algonquin Books of Chapel Hill, 1992, p. 120.

31. American Red Cross website, "Hurricane."

Chapter 4: The Hurricane Hits

32. Quoted in Rick Gore, "Andrew Aftermath," *National Geographic*, April 1993, p. 23.

33. Quoted in Gore, "Andrew Aftermath," p. 23.

34. Jennings, *The Killer Storms*, p. 68.

35. Jennings, *The Killer Storms*, pp. 68–70.

36. Melinda Blanchard and Robert Blanchard, *A Trip to the Beach*. New York: Clarkson Potter, 2000, p. 282.

37. Jennings, *The Killer Storms*, p. 72.

38. Jack Williams et al., "Hurricane Andrew in Florida," *Weatherwise*, December 1992/January 1993. SIRS Knowledge Source, sks.sirs.com.

39. Quoted in Gore, "Andrew Aftermath," p. 22.

40. Longshore, *Encyclopedia of Hurricanes, Typhoons, and Cyclones*, p. 32.

41. Jennings, *The Killer Storms*, p. 80.

42. Rosenfeld, *Eye of the Storm*, pp. 225–26.

43. Barnes, *Florida's Hurricane History*, p. 267.

44. Fox, *Lunatic Wind*, p. 147.

45. Quoted in National Weather Service website, www.nws. noaa.gov/oh/hurricane/inland_flooding.html.

46. Quoted in Action by Churches Together (ACT) Bulletin, "Central America: Hurricane Mitch," Volunteers in Technical Assistance website, www.vita.org/disaster/mitch/0020.html.

Chapter 5: The Aftermath

47. The Disaster Center, "Hurricane Mitch Reports," Disaster Center website, www.disastercenter.com/hurricmr.htm.

48. American Red Cross website, "Responding to Disasters," www.redcross.org/disaster/overview/responding.html.

49. Anonymous, "My Florida Vacation," personal website, members.nbci.com/_XMCM/bflobuzrd/andrew/andrew. html.

50. Barnes, *Florida's Hurricane History*, p. 267.

51. Blanchard and Blanchard, *A Trip to the Beach*, pp. 291–92.

52. Jay Barnes, *North Carolina's Hurricane History*. Chapel Hill: University of North Carolina Press, 1995, p. 186.

53. Fetzer Mills, "Hog Tide," *Sierra*, January/February 2000. EBSCO Information Services, www-us.ebsco.com.

54. Patrick Hughes, "The Great Galveston Hurricane," *Weatherwise,* January/February 1998. Posted on Weatherwise magazine website, www.weatherwise.org/98jfhughes.html.

55. Rocky Mount-Wilson Airport press release, "Rocky Mount-Wilson Airport Plays Major Role in Hurricane Rescue Efforts," Rocky Mount-Wilson Airport website, www.rwiairport.com/what.html.

56. Lawton Chiles, "1993 State of the State Address," Florida Government Services Online website, fcn.state.fl.us/eog/state_of_state/sos_1993.html.

57. Quoted in Michael Parfit, "Living with Natural Hazards," *National Geographic*, July 1998. SIRS Knowledge Source, sks.sirs.com.

58. Quoted in Gore, "Andrew Aftermath," p. 20.

59. Quoted in Elliott Mittler, "A Case Study of Florida's Emergency Management Since Hurricane Andrew," University of Colorado at Boulder website, www.colorado.edu/hazards/wp/wp98.html.

60. Quoted in U.S. Committee on Environment and Public Works, "Federal Response to Hurricane Fran," transcript of the hearing before the Subcommittee on Clean Air, Wetlands, Private Property and Nuclear Safety, October 2, 1996, p. 8.

61. James Bovard, "The Floyd Fiasco," *American Spectator*, November 1999. EBSCO Information Services, www-us.ebsco.com.

62. Elizabeth Razzi, "Scams That Add Insult to Injury," *Kiplinger's Personal Finance Magazine*, May 1994. SIRS Knowledge Source, sks.sirs.com.

63. Quoted in Ted Rose, "What Happened to Our Town?" *Preservation,* July/August 2000. SIRS Knowledge Source, sks.sirs.com

64. Quoted in Charles S. Clark, "Disaster Response," *CQ Researcher*, October 15, 1993. SIRS Knowledge Source, sks.sirs.com

Chapter 6: Taming the Winds

65. Barnes, *Florida's Hurricane History*, p. 300.

66. Fitzpatrick, *Natural Disasters: Hurricanes*, p. 46.

67. Jack Williams, "Ask Jack FAQ," *USA Today Online*, www. usatoday.com/weather/askjack/wfaqhurm.htm.

68. Quoted in AOML website, "Hurricanes and Tropical Meteorology," www.aoml.noaa.gov/general/WWW000/ nhurr00.html.

69. AOML website, "Hurricanes and Tropical Meteorology."

70. William M. Gray et al., "Extended Range Forecast of Atlantic Seasonal Hurricane Activity and US Landfall Strike Probability for 2001," Colorado State University website, tropical.atmos.colostate.edu/forecasts/2001/ fcst2001/index.html.

71. Longshore, *Encyclopedia of Hurricanes, Typhoons, and Cyclones,* p. 234.

72. AOML website, "Hurricanes and Tropical Meteorology."

73. Quoted in Owen Ullmann, "Facing Mother Nature's Fury," *USA Today*, July 24, 2000. SIRS Knowledge Source, sks.sirs.com.

74. Ullmann, "Facing Mother Nature's Fury."

75. Quoted in Ullmann, "Facing Mother Nature's Fury."

76. NOAA et al., "Hurricanes . . . Unleashing Nature's Fury: A Preparedness Guide," U.S. Department of Commerce, March 1994. National Weaher Service website, www.nws. noaa.gov/om/hurrbro.htm.

77. NOAA et al., "Hurricanes."

78. William M. Gray et al., "Summary of 2000 Atlantic Tropical Cyclone Activity and Verification of Authors' Seasonal Activity Forecast," Colorado State University website, typhoon.atmos.colostate.edu/forecasts/2000/ nov2000/index.html.

For Further Reading

Melinda Blanchard and Robert Blanchard, *A Trip to the Beach*. New York: Clarkson Potter, 2000. This delightful book is the true story of two Vermont residents who moved to the tiny island of Anguilla and opened a gourmet restaurant. The book contains some excellent firsthand descriptions of Hurricane Luis.

William Price Fox, *Lunatic Wind: Surviving the Storm of the Century*. Chapel Hill, NC: Algonquin Books of Chapel Hill, 1992. This is the story of Hurricane Hugo. The book includes background information on the region affected by Hugo as well as vivid descriptions of storm survival.

Gary Jennings, *The Killer Storms: Hurricanes, Typhoons, and Tornadoes*. Philadelphia: J. B. Lippincott, 1970. Much of the science in this book is out of date, but the author's simple, colorful descriptions of hurricanes and their effects are marvelous. An extremely enjoyable read.

Sebastian Junger, *The Perfect Storm*. New York: Harper-Perennial, 1997. This is the book on which the blockbuster 2000 movie was based. The author's research is meticulous, and he has packed his book with information about the causes and effects of storms at sea.

Works Consulted

Books

Jay Barnes, *Florida's Hurricane History*. Chapel Hill: University of North Carolina Press, 1998. This book describes the buildup, effects, and aftermath of every significant hurricane in Florida's recorded history. It features all the essential facts about each storm as well as excellent descriptive passages and thoughtful analyses.

Jay Barnes, *North Carolina's Hurricane History*. Chapel Hill: University of North Carolina Press, 1995. Organized in the same way as *Florida's Hurricane History*, this book focuses on hurricanes that have hit North Carolina.

Sharon Maddux Carpenter and Toni Garcia Carpenter, *The Hurricane Handbook*. Lake Buena Vista, FL: Tailored Tours Publications, 1993. A preparation guide for residents of the hurricane belt. It contains detailed information on what to expect, how to prepare, and where to go if a hurricane threatens.

David E. Fisher, *The Scariest Place on Earth: Eye to Eye with Hurricanes*. New York. Random House, 1994. An eyewitness account of the author's experiences during Hurricane Andrew. It is also packed with excellent historical and scientific information about hurricanes in general.

Patrick J. Fitzpatrick, *Natural Disasters: Hurricanes*. Santa Barbara, CA: ABC-CLIO, 1999. An overview of hurricanes, from their formation to their effects to mitigation efforts. Includes an exceptional chronology of U.S. landfalling hurricanes since 1900, with commentary about their impact.

Robert E. Fuerst, *The Typhoon-Hurricane Story*. Rutland, VT: Charles E. Tuttle, 1956. Contains some excellent quotes from survivors of long-ago hurricanes.

David Longshore, *Encyclopedia of Hurricanes, Typhoons, and Cyclones*. New York: Facts On File, 1998. Everything you ever wanted to know about hurricanes, arranged alphabetically by topic. An excellent reference.

Roger A. Pielke, *The Hurricane*. London: Routledge, 1990. A classic in the field of hurricane studies. Often technical, utilizing scientific and mathematical formulas to describe various phenomena, it is also a difficult read. But the quality of the information is exceptionally good.

Jeffrey Rosenfeld, *Eye of the Storm: Inside the World's Deadliest Hurricanes, Tornadoes, and Blizzards*. New York: Plenum Trade, 1999. Written in an engaging narrative style, this book contains a good chapter that touches on the formation, history, effects, and future of hurricanes.

Lyall Watson, *Heaven's Breath: A Natural History of the Wind*. New York: William Morrow, 1984. An impressive collection of information about every wind-related phenomenon throughout human history.

Internet Sources

Action by Churches Together (ACT) Bulletin, "Central America: Hurricane Mitch," Volunteers in Technical Assistance website, www.vita.org/disaster/mitch/0020.html.

Anonymous, "My Florida Vacation," personal website, members.nbci.com/_XMCM/bflobuzrd/andrew/andrew.html.

William Booth, "Hurricane's Fury Left 165 Square Miles Pounded into the Ground," *Washington Post*, August 30, 1992. SIRS Knowledge Source, sks.sirs.com.

James Bovard, "The Floyd Fiasco," *American Spectator*, November 1999. EBSCO Information Services, www-us.ebsco.com.

Chris Cappella, "Dance of the Storms: The Fujiwara Effect," *USA Today Online*, www.usatoday.com/weather/wfujiwha.htm.

Lawton Chiles, "1993 State of the State Address," Florida Government Services Online website, fcn.state.fl.us/eog/state_of_state/sos_1993.html.

Charles S. Clark, "Disaster Response," *CQ Researcher*, October 15, 1993. SIRS Knowledge Source, sks.sirs.com.

The Disaster Center, "Hurricane Mitch Reports," Disaster Center website, www.disastercenter.com/hurricmr.htm.

Earth and Sky Radio Series, "When Hurricanes Collide," June 9, 2000. Earth and Sky website, earthsky.com/2000/esmi000609.html.

Lew Fincher and Bill Read, "The 1943 'Surprise' Hurricane," City of Houston Emergency Management website, www.ci.houston.tx.us/departme/finance/oem/hurricane/.

Sybil Fix, "Pet Shelter Is a Last Resort," Charleston.net Storm Center, www.charleston.net/weather/hurrpets0601.htm.

William M. Gray et al., "Extended Range Forecast of Atlantic Seasonal Hurricane Activity and US Landfall Strike Probability for 2001," Colorado State University website, tropical.atmos.colostate.edu/forecasts/2001/fcst2001/index.html.

William M. Gray et al., "Summary of 2000 Atlantic Tropical Cyclone Activity and Verification of Authors' Seasonal Activity Forecast," Colorado State University website, typhoon.atmos.colostate.edu/forecasts/2000/nov2000/index.html.

David Hancock and Anthony Faiola, "Bigger, Stronger, Closer," *Miami Herald*, August 23, 1992. Accessed through NewsLibrary, www.newslibrary.com.

Patrick Hughes, "The Great Galveston Hurricane," *Weatherwise*, January/February 1998. *Weatherwise* magazine website, www.weatherwise.org/98jfhughes.html.

Christopher W. Landsea, "Frequently Asked Questions: Hurricanes, Typhoons, and Tropical Cyclones," www.aoml.noaa.gov/hrd/tcfaq/tcfaqD.html.

Fetzer Mills, "Hog Tide," *Sierra,* January/February 2000. EBSCO Information Services, www-us.ebsco.com.

Elliott Mittler, "A Case Study of Florida's Emergency Management Since Hurricane Andrew," University of Colorado at Boulder website, www.colorado.edu/hazards/wp/wp98.html.

NOAA et al., "Hurricanes . . . Unleashing Nature's Fury: A Preparedness Guide," U.S. Department of Commerce, March 1994. National Weather Service website, www.nws.noaa.gov/om/hurrbro.htm

Michael Parfit, "Living with Natural Hazards," *National Geographic*, July 1998. SIRS Knowledge Source, sks.sirs.com.

Carl Posey, "Hurricanes: Reaping the Whirlwind," *Omni*, March 1994. Infotrac General Reference Center Gold, library.iacnet.com.

Elizabeth Razzi, "Scams That Add Insult to Injury," *Kiplinger's Personal Finance Magazine*, May 1994. SIRS Knowledge Source, sks.sirs.com

Rocky Mount-Wilson Airport press release, "Rocky Mount-Wilson Airport Plays Major Role in Hurricane Rescue Efforts," Rocky Mount-Wilson Airport website, www.rwiairport.com/what.html.

Ted Rose, "What Happened to Our Town?" *Preservation*, July/August 2000. SIRS Knowledge Source, sks.sirs.com

South Florida Sun-Sentinel, "Finding Shelter for Your Family," posted on Newsday.com, cnews.tribune.com/news/story/0,11 62,newsday-storm-64343,00.html.

Owen Ullmann, "Facing Mother Nature's Fury," *USA Today*, July 24, 2000. SIRS Knowledge Source, sks.sirs.com.

United States Air Force Reserve Weather Reconnaissance Fact Sheet, www.hurricanehunters.com/facrec.htm.

A. B. C. Whipple, "The Hurricane Party at the Richelieu Apartments During Hurricane Camille," excerpted from the book *Storm* and posted on personal website, www.mathstat.usouthal.edu/~lynn/hurricanes/party.html

Jack Williams, "Ask Jack FAQ," *USA Today Online*, www.usa today.com/weather/askjack/wfaqhurm.htm.

Jack Williams et al., "Hurricane Andrew in Florida," *Weatherwise*, December 1992/January 1993. SIRS Knowledge Source, sks. sirs.com.

Christine Winter, "Hurricane Shelter for Pets a Doggone Dilemma," Ferret Friends Disaster Response International website, www.geocities.com/ffdri/friendlyshelters.html.

Periodicals

Charles E. Cobb Jr., "Bangladesh: When the Water Comes," *National Geographic*, June 1993.

Fatty Goodlander, "How to Prepare Your Vessel to Survive a Hurricane in the U.S. Virgin Islands," Virgin Islands Territorial Emergency Management Agency (VITEMA) publication, 1998.

Rick Gore, "Andrew Aftermath," *National Geographic*, April 1993.

Vince Musi, "After the Deluge," *National Geographic*, November 1999.

U.S. Committee on Environment and Public Works, "Federal Response to Hurricane Fran," transcript of the hearing before the Subcommittee on Clean Air, Wetlands, Private Property and Nuclear Safety, October 2, 1996.

Websites

American Red Cross (www.redcross.org). The organization's official website provides information on Red Cross services, policies, history, goals, and more.

Atlantic Oceanographic and Meteorological Laboratory (www.aoml.noaa.gov). The AOML is one of NOAA's research divisions. The organization's website is an excellent source of data, research project summaries, forecasts, flight data, and much more.

Federal Emergency Management Agency (www.fema.gov). FEMA's website describes the agency's function. It includes an informative section on FEMA's disaster management role.

Hurricane Hunters (www.hurricanehunters.com). Learn about the historical and current activities of the Hurricane Hunters on this website.

National Hurricane Center (www.nhc.noaa.gov). The National Hurricane Center is the definitive source of information on Atlantic hurricane activity.

National Weather Service (www.nws.noaa.gov). This site includes information on every type of weather phenomenon, including hurricanes.

NOAA Aircraft Operations Center (www.nc.noaa.gov/aoc). Describes the role of NOAA aircraft and personnel in the hurricane tracking and monitoring effort.

USA Today Online **Hurricane Information** (www.usatoday.com/weather/huricane/whur0.htm). The newspaper has compiled a comprehensive online hurricane information source that contains good basic data, article references, and links to other relevant organizations. A good starting point for hurricane research.

Index

Picture Credits

Cover photo: © Bruce Gordon, 1989/Photo Researchers, Inc.

Agence France Presse/Corbis, 77

AP Photo/Chuck Burton, 64

AP Photo/Andy Newman, 47

AP Photo/Chris O'Meara, 87

AP Photo/Oscar Sosa, 53

© Corbis, 16

FEMA, 49, 50, 55, 68, 70, 74, 75, 78, 79, 81, 91

NOAA, 12, 21, 27, 33, 43, 57, 61

North Wind Picture Archives, 72

© Reuters NewMedia Inc./Corbis, 39

© Galen Rowell/Corbis, 37

Schenectady Museum; Hall of Electrical History Foundation/ Corbis, 83

Martha Schierholz, 8,15, 24

© Stock Montage, 7

© Patrick Ward/Corbis, 92

© Stuart Westmorland/Corbis, 11

About the Author

Kris Hirschmann has written more than forty books for children, mostly on science and nature topics. She is the author of *Lions*, published by KidHaven Books.

Hirschmann is a freelance writer and a member of the Society of Children's Book Writers and Illustrators. She is also the president of The Wordshop, a business that provides a wide variety of writing and editorial services. She holds a bachelor's degree in psychology from Dartmouth College in Hanover, New Hampshire.

Hirschmann lives just outside of Orlando, Florida, with her husband, Michael.